& DIANE RAWLINSON ▪ EARL, ERIC & KURT REDD ▪ SAMUEL LEE ▪ J... ...AN
MARTHA & PAUL R. DUDEN FAMILY ▪ THE SCOTT HINSDALE FAM... ...EY
LY ▪ BOB JOHANNESEN ▪ THE GADSBY FAMILY ▪ DOREEN MORRIS ▪ MERIDEL JUANITA
JOHNSON ▪ MICHAEL & RUTH GUDMAN ▪ MARGARET & LEONARD BENNETT ▪ BRIAN,
BENFIELD FAMILY ▪ RAYMOND M. & NIXON E. (NICK) MUNLY ▪ FRANK LEMMA FAMILY ▪
GERRY FRANK ▪ THE WILLIAM A. KELLY FAMILY ▪ DARLENE IERULLI ▪ SKIP FRANK ▪ FRED
OTTY & TOM LEVAK ▪ JOHN AND BARBARA VAN LANINGHAM ▪ THE WATTS FAMILY ▪ ROBIN
Y GARY ▪ MARGARET JOAN BROCKHAUS ▪ JACK RHINE ▪ ANNAMARIE HOLLAND ▪ JAMES
TS ▪ AL & MARIE SLEIGHT ▪ ROBERT T. & MARGARET MORRIS & FAMILY ▪ ERNIE MATHEWS
& KIRK GLERUM ▪ NORMAN & KATHLEEN HOTZ ▪ HOWARD AND ELZA ZIMMER FAMILY
884 ▪ THE JACK GALLUS FAMILY ▪ DAVE, BARB, MATT, & SUZANNE SLOAN ▪ PEGGY & JOE
KIDS ▪ NATALIE & NICHOLAS McDONALD ▪ JAMES BURCH FAMILY ▪ THE JOYLE C. DAHL
McGUIRE ▪ DAVID, GAIL, & MICHELLE SHEPHERD ▪ BRUCE & ROBYN KELLY ▪ THOMAS P.
▪ DR. LARRY SEMLER ▪ JAMES W. PERKINS ▪ ALEX & AIMEE ZEHNTBAUER-BLOOM ▪ THE
MICHAEL GANN ▪ DON & WILLETTA MORTON ▪ FRANK RAWLINSON ▪ CHAR RAWLINSON
H ▪ NADINE WOOLEY ▪ ANN MARIE SMITH ▪ JULIE SMITH ▪ JOHN & SUZANNE ROBERTI
D, M.D. ▪ DENNIS & LINDA STEIGERWALD ▪ MacTARNAHAN FAMILY ▪ HOWARD & FRAN
▪ PHIL & BARBIE BROWN ▪ WALT & MARIJA KUZMAN ▪ THE CALVIN A. CLEMENTS FAMILY
ELLIS ▪ DENNIS & ANNA MAE DAHLIN ▪ ELLEN Y. BECHTOLD ▪ MARY & PETE MARK ▪ PAUL
DAN ▪ SARAH R. SHERIDAN ▪ ERNEST E. MERGES ▪ EDWARDS MERGES ▪ LINDA O', BLAKE
HILLIP KLUPENGER ▪ GLORIA KLUPENGER ▪ CLARENCE & ELMIRA BEYER ▪ THE MOONEY
ITH ▪ BUD AND JANET LEWIS ▪ MARIANNE & PHILIP FELDMAN ▪ ED & LOURDENE GRAVES
ORDEN FAMILY ▪ THE HOCKLEY FAMILY ▪ ROBERT KROHN ▪ HOWARD ANDREW SONNES
P, M.D. ▪ R.L. JOHNSRUD FAMILY ▪ JOHN H. BOLLONS ▪ DAVID BRUCE MOUNTAIN ▪ THE
RTIN GRANUM ▪ EUGENE D. & SARAH R. EARLEY ▪ DONALD DRYER ▪ WALTER E. GELINSKY
AMILY ▪ GEORGE & MOLLY SPENCER ▪ THE MACY FAMILY ▪ PETER W. STOTT ▪ JIM, EMBRY,
Y ▪ MR. AND MRS. ANDY SMITH ▪ BILL HACKETT ▪ KENNETH J. HALL FAMILY ▪ DONALD
LIN COOK ▪ McCABE & ASSOCIATES ▪ THE A.F. KALBERER FAMILY ▪ BOB & ROBIN MESHER
MILY ▪ THE JOSEPH HEINZ FAMILY ▪ EDNA L. HOLMES ▪ CHARLES B. & CATHRINE S. BOYCE
MARTINE & CHARLES STARR ▪ THE VANCE L. TAYLOR FAMILY ▪ TED & CONNIE GILBERT
ROBERT & KRIS FULTON ▪ CHARLES F. LOEDING, M.D. ▪ ESTELLE BARBUR ▪ THE ALLAN
ALDRIDGE ▪ THE VIAL FAMILY ▪ ROLLO W. AND LEAH M. VAN PELT SR. ▪ THE TIM WEST
T ▪ MAURIE CLARK ▪ THE JAMES P. WHITTEMORE FAMILY ▪ JEFF D. CREARY ▪ BRUCE AND
MOND ▪ THE BALLADEERS ▪ ACCOUNTING ASSOCIATES ▪ JORDAN SCHNITZER ▪ HENRY
Y ▪ THE SALTZMAN FAMILY ▪ JAMES G. SCHNELL ▪ BERKELEY HOLMAN ▪ KENT HIGGON
TT FAMILY ▪ THE LAGESEN FAMILY ▪ PURDY CORPORATION ▪ THE LANGFITT FAMILY ▪
P. EMAHISER, D.M.D. ▪ JAY L. MAXWELL, C.P.A. ▪ DONALD W. GREEN III & FAMILY ▪

Legacy of the Twenty-Six

A Celebration of the First 100 Years of the
MULTNOMAH ATHLETIC CLUB

LEGACY OF THE TWENTY-SIX

A Celebration of the First 100 Years of the
MULTNOMAH ATHLETIC CLUB

KRISTYN McIVOR
JOEL D. FREEMAN
LUANA HELLMANN HILL

With Research by
ERYN L. POTEMPA
DAVID IAN JACKSON

Design by
GRAPHIC MEDIA INC.

Principal Photography by
ROBERT GRAVES
ELLEN M. PAYNE
MICHOLE N. JENSEN
STEVEN BLOCH

The entry to the 1912 Salmon Street clubhouse circa 1941.

Library of Congress Catalog Card Number: 91-060515

Authors: Kristyn McIvor, Joel D. Freeman, Luana Hellmann Hill
Editor: Kristyn McIvor
Title: *Legacy of the Twenty-six*
Subtitle: *A Celebration of the First 100 Years of the Multnomah Athletic Club*

First Edition
Publisher: Multnomah Athletic Club
Publishing Consultant: MEDIAmerica Inc.
Printed by Dynagraphics Inc. of Portland, Oregon
Design by Graphic Media Inc. of Portland, Oregon
Color Separations by ColorXcel Inc. of Portland, Oregon

ISBN 0-9629107-0-8

TABLE OF CONTENTS

ACKNOWLEDGEMENTS

In a collaborative effort such as *Legacy of the Twenty-six*, numerous people took part.

We appreciate the confidence of the Centennial Committee, chaired by Millard McClung from 1986-88 and John Herman from 1989-91, as well as the backing of the board of trustees. We also appreciate the support and understanding of Steve Tidrick and Virgil Kuhls of the management staff.

Hundreds of members provided financial backing; their names are listed on the book's endsheets.

Rolf Glerum, chairman of the book subcommittee, and members Mary McFarland and Ernie Mathews helped define the concept of the book and the team that produced it. Nadine Wooley served early in the project.

Thanks to Rob Fussell and Dick Detweiler of MEDI-America Inc. for handling the details with vendors and for introducing us to Luana Hellmann Hill, a key member of our writing and editing team.

We were fortunate to be able to work with a talented design team from Graphic Media Inc. that included Joe Parker, Janelle Veith, Patty Wisner, Denise Brem, Tom Swearingen and others. Parker provided a particularly personal insight as a MAC member since childhood.

We had the pleasure of working with Cindy Hazen, Armando Herrera and Greg Smith at Dynagraphics Inc., the ever-gracious Lori Spano at ColorXcel Inc. and Ron Walker at Lincoln & Allen. Greg Krolicki's artistry is apparent in all the hand-tinted photos.

Photography is an important part of *Legacy of the Twenty-six*. Photos by founding president A.B. McAlpin appear in early chapters. Many other photographers worked for MAC during the last 100 years, and we acknowledge their contributions. We also thank the many members who loaned us photos or historical items to photograph.

Anecdotes proved essential. Capt. Kenneth McAlpin illuminated his grandfather's character and spirit. And, we enjoyed working with Frances Caskey, the niece of early football player and committee man Frank Harmar. Joe Loprinzi, Lorraine Miller and Becky Nelson were all invaluable in the research. Scrapbooks supplied by club committees and individual members helped with the research. *The Oregonian* library staff and the Multnomah County Library telephone reference department had great attitudes, and the Oregon Historical Society made many scrapbooks the club had donated available to us.

The day-to-day operations of *The Winged M* were ably handled by Ellen M. Payne and the very capable magazine staff: Michole Jensen, Suzanne Hogue and Elise Greenberg. Their professionalism allowed MAC Publications Manager Kristyn McIvor to devote her expertise, creativity and critical eye to transforming *Legacy of the Twenty-six* from mere concept into a work of enduring value.

To Joel Freeman goes a big thanks for his willingness to accept the challenge of researching and writing. We appreciate the help of Stephen D. Beckham, Ph.D., of Lewis & Clark College who referred David Ian Jackson and Eryn L. Potempa to us as interns. Well-versed in research, both became staff members through the end of the project.

Many thanks also to Jill Wilson who was on call for grammatical questions and proofreading, as well as to Bill Fisher for final proofreading.

Most importantly, to our friends and families, thank you all for your patience and compassion.

K.M., J.D.F., L.H.H.

INTRODUCTION

"Now, devotees may argue that one sport or game is inherently better than another. For me," John Keating says to his students in the movie *Dead Poets Society,* "sport is actually a chance for us to have other human beings push us to excel."

Legacy of the Twenty-six challenged all involved to excel. The club's history is full and rich; carving it from encyclopedic proportions to book size required sacrifice and discipline.

The history of the Multnomah Athletic Club is intimately entwined with the history of sport as well as the history of Portland and its institutions. Luminaries such as Teddy Roosevelt, Taft, Harding and Coolidge all visited the club. Memories carry these historic moments into the future.

The desire to leave an accurate historical record drove the research effort. We corrected some of the records used for reference. Just one of many instances is the case of a wrestler named Oscar Franzke. His last name was misspelled in a wrestling history. *Winged M* magazines referred to him as Oscar but the board minutes called him Otto. Normally, we would assume the board minutes would be the most accurate source. Fortunately, fate smiled on us; Franzke's granddaughter, Pam Jones, contacted the research staff and we were able to correct his first name just before the book was printed.

Sometimes, there were confusing coincidences. There really were two "Dudley Clarks." The first, an early football player who went on to an acting career, spelled his last name with an e. The other, a club president, was just plain old Clark. Ladies' Annex and Women's Annex as well as Men's Bar and Men's Grille were used interchangeably.

Defining a champion was a challenge. During the club's first decades, outstanding athletes set record after record. By the club's centennial year, the sheer magnitude of those achieving national stature caused us to mention only those who ranked first and second. Yet, even with this restrictive guideline, the champions crowd six full pages in the final chapter.

If we could select only one person as the epitome of the legacy of the Multnomah Athletic Club's founders, it would be Dr. Collister Wheeler, hands down. As an athlete, a former MAC resident and a former trustee, Collie, 97, serves as a wonderful resource. Through his example, he pushes others to excel.

Collie is the modern-day counterpart to Frank Watkins. Watkins' scrapbooks and his history of the first 25 years of the club were invaluable resources that captured much that would otherwise be lost.

The Multnomah Athletic Club, throughout its first century, was a place of sportsmanship, not just athleticism. There was dignified honor in competing gallantly. It was the camaraderie, not just the sport. From member to member, generation to generation, these values continue through fine example.

All members of the Multnomah Athletic Club, past, present and future, can appreciate that they and the club staff make MAC a fun, family-feeling institution that will continue to enrich the lives of all who have contact with it. The challenge to each other is to excel. This is your legacy.

Kristyn McIvor
Editor

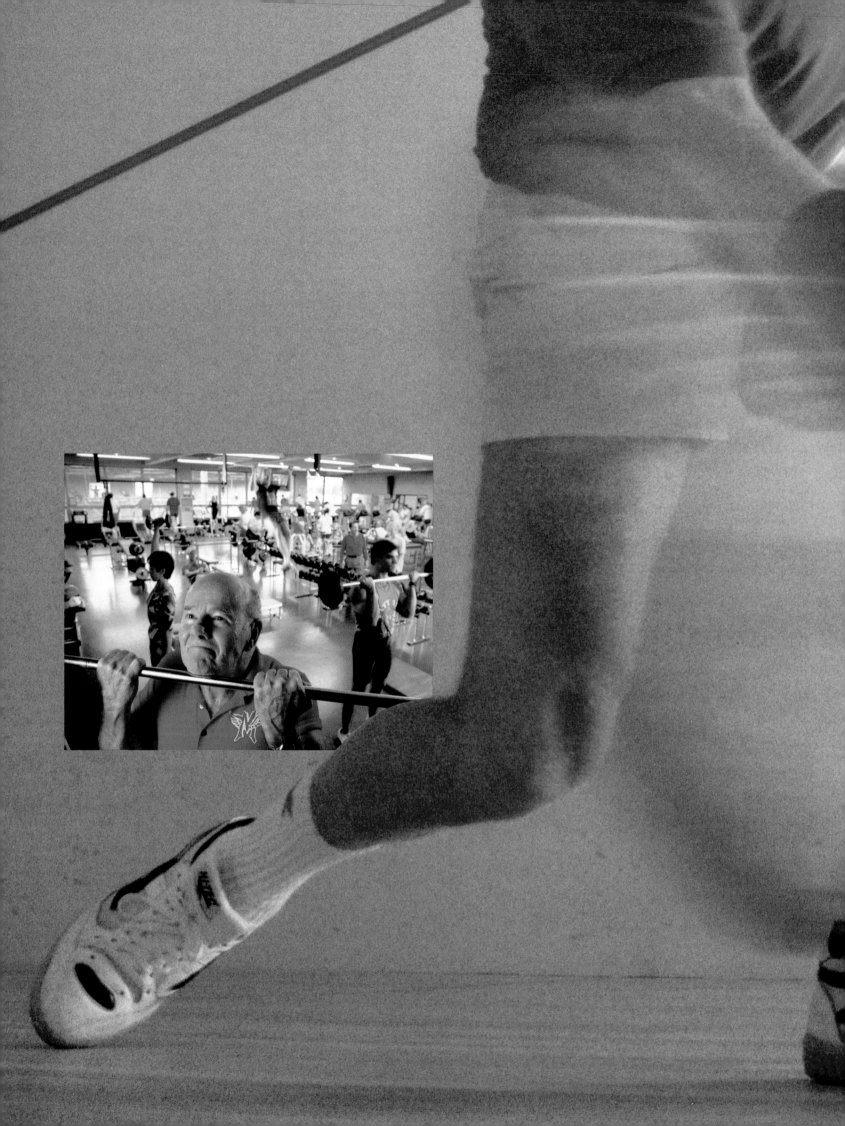

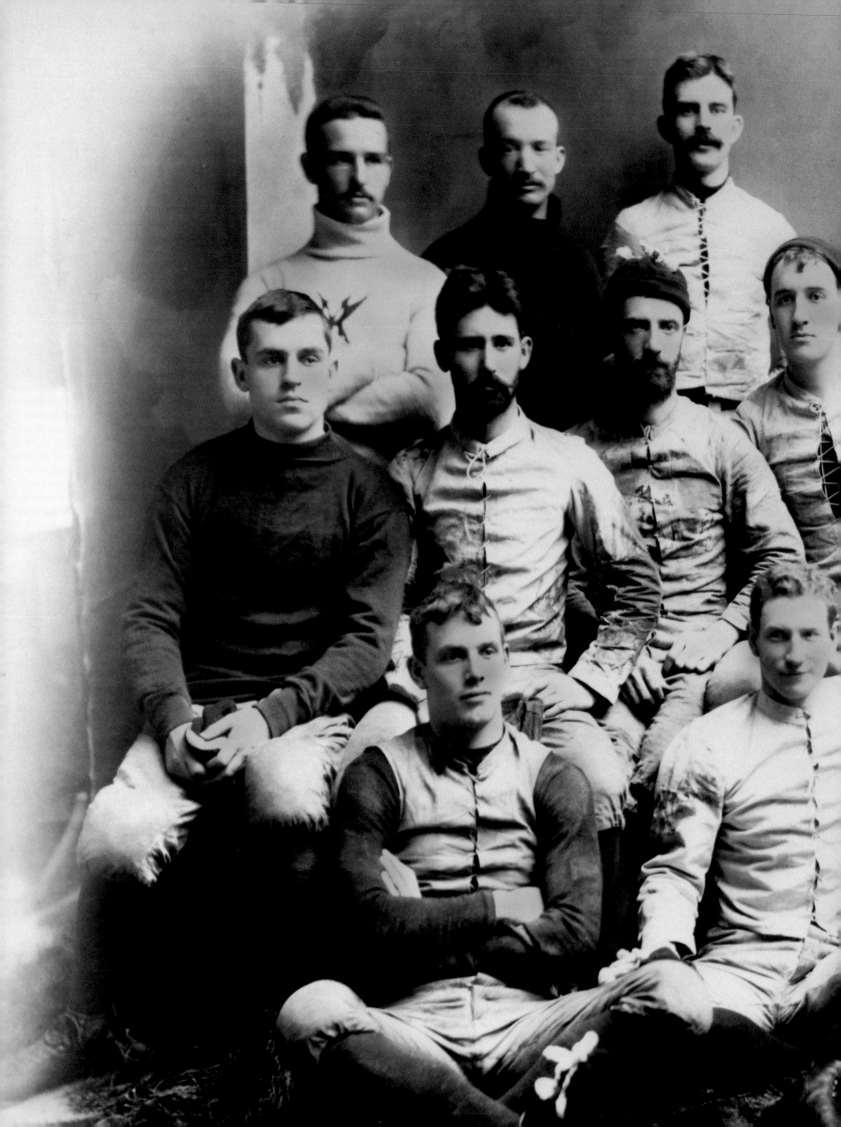

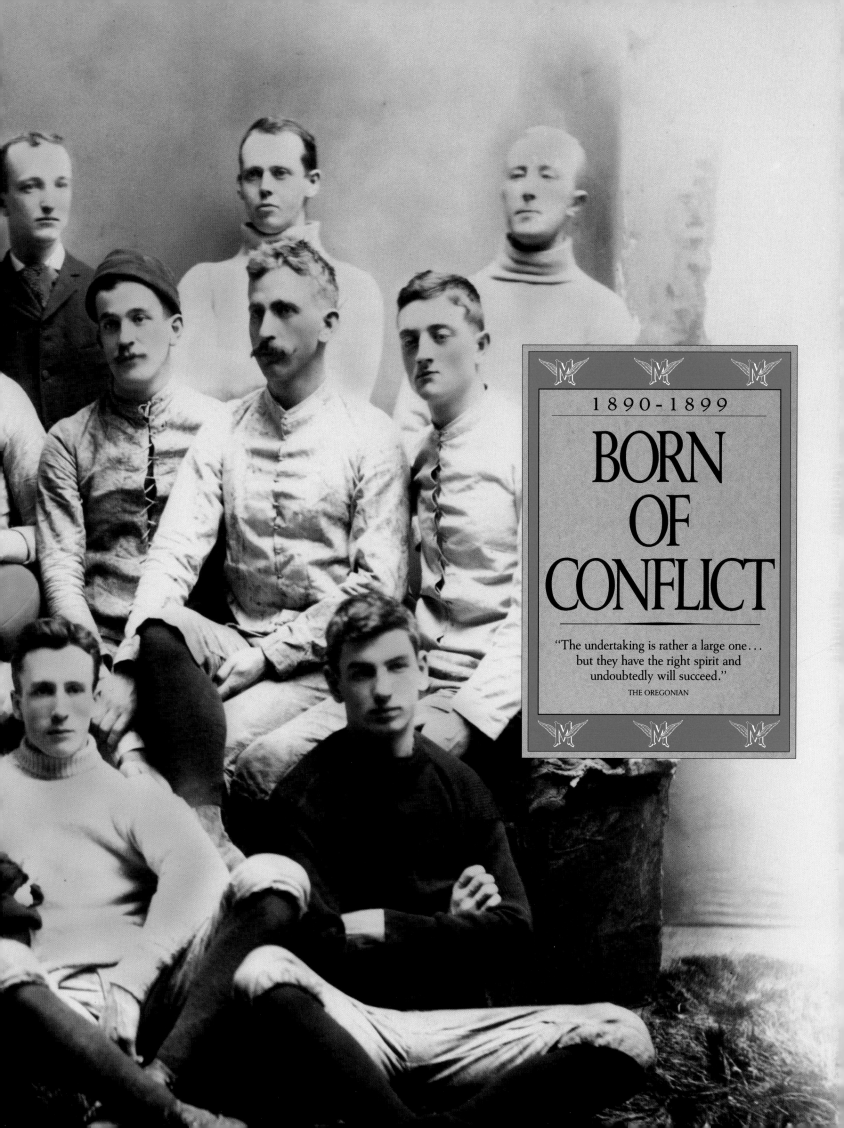

1890-1899

BORN
OF
CONFLICT

"The undertaking is rather a large one...
but they have the right spirit and
undoubtedly will succeed."

THE OREGONIAN

MAC
TIMELINE

1890

OREGON POPULATION IS 317,704
RUBBER SURGICAL GLOVES FIRST USED
AT JOHNS HOPKINS HOSPITAL

1891

ZIPPER INVENTED
THE LONGEST ELECTRIC STREETCAR
SERVICE IN PORTLAND, "THE
METROPOLITAN," RUNS SIX MILES FROM
NORTHWEST SECOND AND GLISAN
TO THE RIVERVIEW CEMETERY

1892

FERRIS WHEEL INTRODUCED

1893

SALEM-TO-PORTLAND PHONE
EXCHANGE OPENS
HENRY FORD BUILDS HIS FIRST CAR

1894

GEORGE HARDIN BECOMES PORTLAND'S
FIRST BLACK POLICE OFFICER
VOLLEYBALL INVENTED
ROENTGEN DISCOVERS X-RAYS
KING C. GILLETTE INVENTS THE
SAFETY RAZOR

1896

FIRST MODERN OLYMPIAD,
ATHENS, GREECE
UNION STATION BUILT
FIRST MOVING PICTURE ON A PUBLIC
SCREEN IN NEW YORK CITY

1898

MAAC TENNIS COURTS BUILT

1899

HENRY WEMME BRINGS FIRST AUTO,
STANLEY STEAMER, TO PORTLAND
MCKINLEY BECOMES FIRST PRESIDENT
TO RIDE IN AN AUTOMOBILE,
A STANLEY STEAMER

"Opposition forces" is the way *The Oregonian* described them. Led by photographer Arthur B. McAlpin, 34, the 26 insisted upon a $10 initiation fee while the others among the 150 or so present wanted to offer only old tattered football uniforms as payment.

A new alliance for amateur sports was the purpose of the meeting. Portland was ready. Weeks of preliminary talks, public debate and preparations showed that. The popularity of the Portland Football and Cricket Club proved that it was so. All that was lacking was the formality of incorporation, and the setting for that event had been arranged – Tuesday evening, February 24, 1891, at Columbia Hall.

But "...the hall was filled with two rival factions," *The Sunday Oregonian* reported. "The meeting was not as harmonious as some of its most ardent supporters would have liked it."

The incompatibility of the 150 men intensified and the meeting adjourned in chaos. McAlpin, an independent-minded pragmatist, located the building superintendent and immediately rented the hall. He and the other dissidents quickly elected their own interim board and chose a name. Articles of incorporation were drafted on the 26th and, two days later, filed in Salem. The Multnomah Amateur Athletic Club was born.

NEW LEISURE TIME BRINGS SPORTS TO MASSES

Sport was new.

Daily life had changed in the years following the Civil War. The Industrial Revolution and its wealth created leisure time for classes other than the rich. Advances in communication and travel brought fresh ideas from afar. Americans accepted the Germanic belief that physical activity could improve both the individual and society; the English passion for fair competition was embraced. Games evolved into sport.

The modern sports era blossomed in the 1890s, captivating the American public. Games now taken for granted – football, baseball, basketball, volleyball, tennis, bowling – were newly introduced, reformed or legitimized. Sports advocates formed associations of their own.

In 1891, of all the West Coast cities, Portland, population 50,000-plus, was second only to San Francisco in wealth and population. It had a diverse social climate, great aspirations and for the past five years, football. Proponents

CHAPTER OPENING PHOTO: Football provided the impetus for forming the Multnomah Amateur Athletic Club. Members of its first team were: top, E.P. Dosch, A.B. McAlpin, C. Lewis, Manager T.S. Brooke, W.H. Chapin, W. Lipman; middle, R. Green, W.A. Montgomery, J. Gavin, J. Savage, R.L. Glisan, W.A. Holt, H. Fiske; front, W.L. Kendall, A.M. Ellsworth, C.E. McDonnell, M. Brooke.

Portland in 1903. Chapman Street clubhouse, opened in July 1900, is in lower left corner next to the Exposition and Recreation Building.

ARTHUR BANCROFT MCALPIN

For Arthur B. McAlpin, founding president of MAAC, leadership was a matter of principle and initiative, not charisma. It was the power of his example that led 25 other men in rebellion to form the club.

Great personal initiative was ingrained in McAlpin's character. Born near Philadelphia on September 21, 1856, to a suffragist mother and minister-turned-lawyer father, McAlpin was left on his own in San Francisco at age 12 when his mother and (now) stepfather returned to the East to pursue a social cause.

At 28, self-educated and a self-taught photographer, McAlpin arrived in Portland carrying only a suitcase and his studio equipment. His days riding shotgun for Wells Fargo over, he came seeking opportunity in the young city.

The tall, lanky McAlpin (5 feet 11 inches, 145 pounds) was an accomplished if not outstanding athlete. He played football until he was 37, tennis

(continued)

of the game, primarily members of the Portland Football and Cricket Club, wanted to expand local athletic opportunities. So, in early February, they invited area enthusiasts to forge a new alliance.

Organizers assured the press and public this would be no "Down Town Athletic Club," the infamous New York boxing gymnasium whose president bit off a political challenger's ear. The proposed Portland Amateur Athletic Club would instead be devoted to physical and social advancement — "strictly first-class...no professional athlete will be allowed."

The meeting's eventual outcome was not as originally planned, but the original plan could not have turned out so well.

McAlpin later recalled: "When we started the club...so many fight clubs were being organized in San Francisco. We organized strictly as an amateur club, however. No liquors were allowed and no gambling was permitted. We then went around to such men as the Ladds, the Corbetts and Cookingham. It was hard to get men of such caliber [to join], but we finally succeeded."

By March 26, membership stood at 200, and the initiation fee was raised to $25.

On April 4, third-floor club rooms opened on Southwest Second Avenue between Yamhill and Morrison. The leased space had a gymnasium with

MCALPIN cont'd.

into his 80s. He was one of the first three climbers to ascend Mount Hood's north face. Cyclist and oarsman, squash racquets expert and swimmer, he was the consummate sportsman.

McAlpin served two terms (1891, 1893) as club president, chaired numerous committees and counseled trustees for 50-plus years. Later, he was manager of the Multnomah Golf Club and assistant manager at MAAC.

He started the Father-Son Dinner in 1931. According to his grandson, Captain Kenneth McAlpin, of all his accomplishments, he was proudest of his work with young people. Working with youth, he felt, kept him young.

McAlpin's 90th birthday was feted throughout the city. Congratulations included a telegram from London from George Bernard Shaw, also 90. Six months later, after a short illness, McAlpin died.

In 1991, an award named for McAlpin was created to honor a member for extraordinary service and significant contributions to the club. Criteria included leadership and continued dedication as well as commitment to the quality and type of social activities offered at the club.

The first McAlpin Award honored Jeff Gudman. Since 1980, Gudman, 36, has assisted many club committees: budget and finance, property, centennial, aquatics, athletic, entertainment and the social advisory council. His dedication to the club is apparent — he has served simultaneously on two or three committees during the last six years and has completed several special project assignments as well.

"the best floor in the city," a carpeted reading room, a billiard room with three tables and a locker area with showers. *The Oregonian* reported, "All of the appliances are of the most modern make, so that the gymnasium will be a model one in every particular."

By May 15, athletic apparatus worth $800, ordered from Spalding in Chicago, had been installed. "Professor" Herman Boos had been hired as gymnastics instructor. Club bylaws were amended to allow "junior guests" to use the facilities. The first general meeting of the full membership returned the interim board intact, save one member who had left the city. The Multnomah Amateur Athletic Club was ready to begin activities in earnest.

EAGER SPORTSMEN JUMP INTO ACTION

Multnomah wasted no time joining the athletic fray. W. L. Murray, later the club's first swimming instructor and Turkish bath attendant, was its first competitor, entering the Oregon National Guard's spring games at the Armory. A club baseball team was organized in early June.

When MAAC announced its first fall games, the impact was felt throughout the Northwest. Many events were to make their first showing in the city, and the novelty of such a large-scale competition was unmistakable. Athletes from Salt Lake City, Seattle, Oakland, and Victoria and

First home of MAAC was on the upper floor of the building at center. Although it was razed, the remainder of the block still stands on Southwest Second between Yamhill and Morrison.

Vancouver, British Columbia, competed for "elegant gold and silver medals... some costing as much as $30."

The Oregonian promised the "auspicious occasion" would "remind one...of the ancient Romans and the gladiators...and it is certain that no less than 5,000 people will attend the games. It will...give amateur athletic sports an upward push as a pure and honorable pastime." Indeed it did. At least two track meets were held annually until 1897.

In October 1891, Multnomah fielded its first football squad. On Halloween day, the Jack Savage-led Winged M team lost a practice game to the

▶ *page 22*

FIRST BOARD OF TRUSTEES OF M.A.A.C.

1891 to 1892

L.J.GOLDSMITH   B.L.CARR   HERBERT WILSON

SECRETARY W.H.CHAPIN   VICE PRESIDENT J.W.PADDOCK   PRESIDENT A.B.McALPIN   TREASURER C.L.BICKEL

J.W.McFALL   R.P.EFFINGER   W.F.LIPMAN   H.E.JUDGE

PORTLAND, OREGON

The first Board of Trustees, headed by President A.B. McAlpin, included Vice President John W. Paddock, Secretary W.H. Chapin, Treasurer George L. Bickel, Louis J. Goldsmith, Bruce L. Carr, Herbert Wilson, J.W.P. McFall, R.P. Effinger, William F. Lipman and H.E. Judge. Others who made up the original members were: T.D. Barton, B.N. Bowman, John B. Coe, Felix Friedlander, Edward N. Gaudron, Hugo B. Goldsmith, Melvin Goldsmith, M.L. Kline, Julius C. Lang, I.N. Lipman, Dr. Aeneas E. Mackay, Richard Miller, W.P. Prindle, Alfred Robertson, and Milton Wasserman. Trustee Paddock, not one of the original 26, replaced B.L. Hutchins when Hutchins moved from Portland. Of the original 26 members, 17 were football players.

McAlpin & Lamb

MULTNOMAH

Deeply impressed by the young club's solvent, serious and sober attitude, W.S. Ladd had a clubhouse built at Southwest 10th and Yamhill. With social rooms richly decorated in scarlet velours, it also had a covered squash-tennis/handball court, gymnasium with running track, swimming tank, bowling lanes and 350 lockers. Opened October 18, 1893, its furnished value was $60,000.

In the crisp autumn of 1890, local football players gathered at the foot of Lincoln Street in response to Jack Caruthers' notice in The Oregonian. Among them were Charles McDonnell, a founder of the Portland Football and Cricket Club; John Gavin, Will Lipman and Ray Green.

Gavin, who learned football at Yale, introduced the game locally in 1886 at Bishop Scott Academy. But BSA played rugby and association football (soccer)—the ''intercollegiate'' rules weren't formed until 1888.

Lipman and Green insisted they play the new version, and so it was. Informal games with BSA led to the fateful meetings at Columbia Hall in early 1891. Gavin, Caruthers and the rest would soon wear MAAC's crimson and white.

That November, MAAC won its first official game against the Tacoma Athletic Club, beginning a dynasty that lasted 35 years.

Football of the 1890s was built around three-play, five-yard scrimmages. Pushing, pulling, carrying and hurling the ball-carrier were legal. Linesmen's belts had loops for teammates to grab. Plays ended only when the ball-carrier cried ''down.'' Players wore tight canvas lace-up uniforms and boots with leather cleats, occasionally adding nose guards, cricket shin guards and pot holders for pads. Though helmets appeared in 1895, most players opted for the protection of ''football hair,'' long and parted in the middle.

The first three short seasons stoked club and Portland interest. Amherst's Frank Raley, captain of the 1892 MAAC team, introduced

By 1898, football uniforms included padded pants, but still no helmets. The Spanish-American War drew many club athletes away from playing fields. This ''replacement'' team started a dynasty, vanquishing foes from San Francisco to Seattle. Considered extremely heavy, most players weighed about 160. They included: Fred Vila, Fred ''Cinch'' Hamilton, Arthur Downs, Ed Davey, W. P. Sinnott, H. Smith, Karl Lively, Spike Young, Billie Jordan, George McMillen, LeConie Stiles, Frank Harmar, W.B. Fletcher.

Fullback W.B. Fletcher as MAAC captain 1898. He led several championship teams at the turn of the century. Fletcher's sons, Robert M. and William, and grandchildren, Mike, Bryn and Robert L., are members.

interference and plays like the V-trick and turtleback to the Pacific Northwest. In 1893, Joseph H. Smith's game-winning last-minute drop kick was the first of many such plays, earning him regional fame as "the Only Joe." That year the first club juniors' football team won an undefeated season.

Portland's first "big game," January 1, 1894, against Stanford at Multnomah Field, launched a 25-year rivalry. As 5,000 watched, even the coaching of Yale legend "Pudge" Heffelfinger couldn't save MAAC from the Cardinals' new flying wedge formation. MAAC fell 16-0.

With football in vogue, MAAC met club and college opponents throughout the West.

By 1905, football violence prompted Congress to talk of outlawing the game. MAAC had its share — "Cinch" Hamilton died from game injuries in the late '90s. With President Teddy Roosevelt's persuasion, colleges banned momentum mass plays. The revolutionary forward pass was introduced; speed and deception were foremost.

The old ways had served MAAC well, though. Its record through 1905 was formidable: 58 wins, 17 losses and 13 ties; 921 points for, 310 against; and six undefeated seasons, including two

No sign yet of barkdust-filled bare patches on the field during this early season Saturday afternoon game.

in which their foes were all held scoreless. Detractors complained of "Multnomah luck"; fans replied that "Multnomah pluck" won those games. New rules or not, Multnomah would continue to move the ball downfield.

Club junior teams trained future greats. This 1893 team included Frank Harmar, middle row, third from left; Frank Watkins and Bert Kerrigan, both seated lower right, who left indelible stamps on club history.

CAP THE DOG

Club mascot Cap, Fred Andrews'
30-pound pit bull, earned fame among
mid-1890s club members for his true
Multnomah spirit. On November 1,
1895, MAAC suffered its worst foot-
ball defeat yet, 40-0, to Oakland's
Reliance Athletic Club, apparently
upsetting Cap enough to fight with an
unaffiliated 150-pound Great Dane.

Frank Watkins wrote, "Cap's
courage exceeded his judgment. When
they were separated, for Cap would
never quit, he was shy a large piece of
his neck but his fighting heart was still
all there." In 1898, Cap's contribution
was acknowledged by the gift of a collar
with an engraved silver nameplate.

experienced Bishop Scott Academy team. Since the BSA season had concluded, Multnomah wisely incorporated most of the school's team into its own before accepting a challenge from the Tacoma Athletic Club. The game ended in favor of Multnomah, and Tacoma immediately requested a January 1 rematch at home.

As MAAC's team marched down the middle of Tacoma's Pacific Avenue, 60 clubmen joined in. But after learning a Tacoma man had played professional baseball, Multnomah threatened to boycott. Under the strict rules of the day, his play jeopardized the amateur status of both teams. The Tacoma player withdrew and the game proceeded to a Multnomah victory.

At Multnomah's spring 1892 handicap track meet, football-leader Savage became the first club member to set a West Coast record. Later, in September 1894, MAAC hosted the first track meet of the newly organized Pacific Northwest Association. It featured the club's first great track team: Bert Kerrigan, E.E. Morgan, Bill Tallant and others.

Still, MAAC's athletic status on the West Coast was not secured until a June 1896 dual invitational meet with San Francisco's Olympic Club. Kerrigan, 5 feet 4 inches, set an unofficial world record in the high jump that stood for 20 years. Tallant set the coast record for the mile by beating the current record holder, an Olympic man. MAAC won the meet; the sportsmanship extended by both teams still endures as a friendly rivalry today.

Success suited Multnomah. Within six months of its inception, membership had grown so dramatically that the downtown facilities expanded to the third floor of an adjacent building. Membership grew to 400 by 1892, straining capacity. Again club trustees approached community leaders for support; again it was granted.

"Happy we were," said McAlpin, "when W.S. Ladd spent nearly $40,000 in putting up a clubhouse for us." With the payment of $400 a month rent guaranteed by 14 of the club's wealthier members, a five-year renewable lease was signed. Multnomah would have its first clubhouse at the corner of Southwest 10th and Yamhill, where the county library now stands.

By early 1893, MAAC also had its own athletic field. Five acres of pasture were leased in Tanner Creek Gulch, next to the huge Exposition Building. Once

The bicycling craze of the 1890s meant many Multnomah men made their way on wheels. George ''Musical'' Foss, left, and A.B. McAlpin pose before a tandem for an 1895 self-portrait. McAlpin holds a shutter-release device behind his back; the cord trails near the rear bike wheel.

Bicycle races were part of many track meets of the day.

SOMETIME BEFORE 1900, JAMES
HONEYMAN WAS AWARDED THIS MEDAL
FOR SCORING 97 IN MAAC ROD & GUN
CLUB MARKSMANSHIP COMPETITION. THE
PIN, DONATED BY HIS SON RONALD J.
HONEYMAN, IS ONE OF THE MORE ORNATE
MEDALS TYPICAL OF THOSE AWARDED
DURING THE EARLY YEARS OF THE CLUB.

HONEYMAN'S DESCENDANTS HAVE
CONTINUED THEIR AFFILIATION WITH THE
CLUB. HIS SON, RONALD J., SERVED AS
CLUB PRESIDENT IN 1941. RONALD J.'S
SON, RONALD C., WAS ALSO A CLUB
TRUSTEE. HE WAS ELECTED TREASURER
IN 1969. FOURTH GENERATION MEMBERS
ARE CRAIG AND JEFF HONEYMAN
AND JANE RUDE.

the site of Daniel Lownsdale's 1840s tannery, Multnomah Field featured a natural amphitheater perfect for athletic use. A small grandstand was constructed in the northwest corner close to the end of the field. In the southwest corner stood the training house, where athletes dressed and showered, or had pre-game rubdowns with a concoction of goose grease, witch hazel and alcohol.

Changes in membership matched the physical changes. In 1892, sons and brothers of members and nominees with no immediate relatives could apply for junior membership. Women were soon admitted too. The Board minutes of April 3, 1894, tidily announced: "Arrangements having been completed... to admit ladies to the use of the Club house [sic] on certain week days," at first two mornings per week. So many nominations were received for the Ladies Annex that a special committee was established to process the memberships.

NEW SPORTS GAIN APPEAL

The invention of the "safety" bicycle in the 1890s started a national cycling boom, and Multnomah succumbed to the trend. Track meets regularly featured "wheelmen." By 1896, cycling's peak year, the competitions featured both amateur and touring professional riders. MAAC also spawned recreational cycling groups such as the "Early Birds."

MAAC sports reflected the British influence on the Northwest. A June 22, 1895, cricket team poses in front of the fieldhouse in the southwest corner of Multnomah Field.

Baseball was a part of club activities from the first year. In both 1893 and 1895, Joe Smith led a MAAC squad to the Northwest championship. The '95 victory over PAAC sparked a torchlight and fireworks parade through downtown. Yet, the blood rivals set aside their differences long enough to play as a single team that October in an exhibition against a traveling team of major leaguers. Mercifully, the game was called for darkness as the MAAC/PAAC team trailed 22-4. Professional baseball grew in favor with players and fans alike, and interclub baseball had all but disappeared by 1907.

Record setting high-jumper Bert Kerrigan clears the handkerchief-flagged bar at the 1895 PNA championships.

The Spanish-American War also took a toll on amateur athletics at MAAC and other clubs, with prime sportsmen leaving for the army. But by then MAAC's social side had come to life. Ladies' nights, exhibitions and "smokers" kept Multnomah entertained. Club-sponsored mandolin and glee clubs performed around town, as did Professor Youngman's banjo and guitar orchestra. The wartime absence of established athletes prepared younger players to create a new Multnomah football dynasty.

Handball and cocked hat bowling surged in popularity. In 1896, yet another new game, basketball — played by both sexes — made its club debut. Tennis had been played in Portland at least since 1892, most notably by the club's Joe Smith and Fred Andrews, contestants at the 1894 PNA finals in Tacoma.

Thus, the club ended its first decade on solid ground. The founders' early insistence on an initiation fee had paid multiple dividends. Working capital and a more egalitarian membership philosophy were assured. Multnomah was the largest, most active and most ethnically diverse club of any in Portland, enjoying both public and private favor.

COCKED HAT BOWLING

More difficult than 10-pins, cocked hat bowling — named for the shape of a tricorn or "cocked" hat — briefly took the Northwest by storm. Three squat, fat bowling pins set in a triangle, 36 inches apart, had to be knocked down by a grapefruit-sized ball.

According to club member Frank Watkins, from 1895 to 1898, "fully 90 percent of the membership secured to the club...was due to 'Cocked Hat.' " Since club alleys charged per game, cocked hat "probably did as much or more than any other one branch of sport to pull us out."

With four of Portland's 80 cocked hat lanes, the club fielded many men's, women's, and coed teams and engaged in inter-club, city, and regional contests with teams from Seattle, Astoria, Albany and The Dalles. Known for its running delivery and a fast throw, MAAC captured the American Cocked Hat Association championship in 1895.

Still, the sport never caught on east of St. Louis, and by 1907 it had died out, to be replaced by 10-pins.

Off the playing fields and out of the locker room, the club's early athletes showed another kind of talent — for dramatic humor. During the 1890s and early 1900s, they staged "farcical, spectacular, terpsichorean musical burlesques" that gave audiences "the glorious opportunity of seeing the men they admire dressed in the garb of ballet girls, leading ladies, and pretty lasses."

Performed at the city's leading theaters, the Marquam Grand and Heilig, these elaborate, festive public entertainments usually shared the common purpose of raising funds to outfit the club. (An added performance of Mr. & Mrs. Cleopatra *was also presented following the 1894 flood "for the benefit of the flood sufferers.") The 1914* Colonial Beaux and Belles in Dixieland *was "to raise money for new handball courts." The 1903 production of* The Wizard of the Nile *netted the goodly sum of $740.58 — more than*

half the annual income of the average household, and a tidy profit, considering ticket prices ranged from 25 cents for gallery seats to $1 for the main floor, and costumes, sets and programs were done in fine style.

Casting followed the Shakespearean tradition of men only, though dances were sometimes choreographed by the leading female performers of traveling vaudeville troupes. Their help led to better staging, acting, and singing to tie the farcical plot lines together. But, as an account of one performance said, "The play is not so much the thing as are the players."

Enthusiastic audiences enjoyed the sight of 200-pound Ivan Humason and 6-foot-3-inch, 225-pound football captain Jack Savage as "babes" in the club's 1893 theatrical debut, Babes in the Woods. *Dan Malarkey "swept the stage in his close-fitting black gown with its tight-laced waist," said* The Evening Telegram, *and the assembly "breathlessly watched the graceful glide and*

Dom Zan, here as one of the Babes in the Woods, *provided the RBI that won MAAC's first baseball game on June 6, 1891, against Company I, First Regiment, of the Oregon National Guard.*

high kicking'' of a seven-man ballet featuring such early club luminaries as Will Lipman.

Mr. & Mrs. Cleopatra featured ''occasional entrances of Antony's eight forlorn fiances'' along with ballets and army marches. It was followed in 1895 by the ''tragedy'' of The Hawaiian King Pro Tem, a prophetic satire about politics and Hawaii's annexation to the United States. Its memorable acts included a ''soubrettes chorus by eight little precocious boys'' dressed as girls, a Napoleon ballet and ''Royal Russian acrobats.''

Thanks to studio photographs of the mustachioed young cast members in their costumes (taken by club leader A.B. McAlpin), it is possible to picture the early days, when club members were good sports on the vaudeville stage as well as the playing field.

Male members cast for the Grand Napoleon Ballet from the 1895 satire The Hawaiian King Pro Tem, *were: top, H.F. Gaylord, H.L. Gaylord, Alex DeFrance; below, W.H. Northrup, E.H. Geary, F.D. Reames, E.B. Sterling and H.L. Kreiss.*

MAC

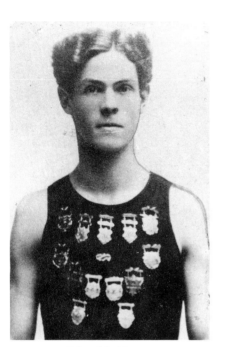

Edward E. Morgan

Joseph Harker Smith

From the first modern Olympics in 1896 evolved the ideal of a champion as an athlete of national or international prominence. Yet the early Winged M athletes lived by a more regional code. To speak of a champion of this period is to acknowledge someone who stood out often in games or meets, or who challenged the most men and won the most matches.

Record-setting took place at all levels of competition and needed only to be proclaimed by the athlete and one other witness. The names of the club's first champions usually pepper accounts of several sports, not just one.

Billy Lasswell was "the fastest 220 and 440 man in the Northwest in his day and one of the best halfbacks the club has ever had," Frank Watkins wrote in 1916. "He was a wonderfully strong man for his size, being splendidly built and weighing about 165 stripped."

Billy Lasswell

Lasswell left MAAC for the famed football team, the Copper Kings of Butte, Montana, where he died in 1900.

In the mile run, *William Tallant* earned renown for Multnomah, setting the PNA record in 1895 with a time of 4:40.8 and taking the 1896 Pacific Coast record. "Peter Grant had trained [Tallant] by running over the Astoria hills and when he put on a pair of spiked shoes and got on a level track it was so easy for him that he could not help winning...," Watkins said.

Discovered at the 1896 Pacific Coast championships was *Frank Coyne*, who took the 440-yard run and "never lost a scratch 440 for us," according to *The Winged M*. A veteran of the Spanish-American War, Coyne remained in the Philippines; he died in 1907.

Frank Coyne

William Tallant

Edward E. Morgan excelled in several sports, chief among them track and football. From his decathlon win in 1893, "Mr. Morgan never lost in a track event," a 1965 tribute in *The Winged M* read; three times he took the Reed Cup, an intramural competition for best club athlete, earning permanent possession. He also played catcher for the 1891 baseball team. A spirited, tenacious competitor, Morgan was once kicked in the head during a football game lost to Seattle. After continuing to play helmetless, he awoke from an amnesiac stupor while walking to a theater four hours later. In 1928, MAAC made the gentleman farmer from Gaston an honorary life member.

Life member *Joseph Harker Smith* was regionally famed as "The Only Joe" because of his "remarkable ability to 'deliver the goods' for the club in a pinch." He played baseball, football — both rugby and intercollegiate — was a football captain, ran track, played expert billiards and bowled. In 1894, with tennis in its infancy, Smith and Fred Andrews reached the PNA finals in Tacoma.

The name of *Herbert Greenland* was synonymous with wrestling in the club's early years. After besting perennial Olympic Club rival Tiv Kreling, Greenland held the Pacific Coast lightweight amateur championship for five years. His widely admired sense of sportsmanship led him to hold comment on a questionable call that finally cost him his title. The longtime Portland tailor was the first club member voted honorary life membership.

Herbert Greenland

1900-1909

A PLACE TO CALL HOME

"Multnomah is open to all.
It is made up of the people who are
interested in the welfare of Portland..."

*FROM A LETTER TO THE EDITOR OF
THE TELEGRAM, JANUARY 6, 1906*

The timing was perfect. In June 1899, MAAC membership was increasing dramatically, thanks to an active campaign. The lease on the Southwest 10th and Yamhill property would expire in six months; W.S. Ladd wanted to donate the buildings to the Portland Academy. The Scottish American Investment Corporation, owners of Multnomah Field, had received an offer on a section of that land, but the club had first rights. Destiny called: despite the distance from city center, MAAC would buy the field and build a new clubhouse.

After MAAC raised $10,000 through bond sales, trustee Dan Moore, a hotel developer, negotiated the deal. The club purchased the field at $33,000, guaranteeing to construct a clubhouse costing not less than $22,000, with the King family financing the package at 6 percent. Various members were then sent East to study club facilities there.

The Exposition Building, built in 1887 for $80,000, was located on the north end of Multnomah Field. When it burned in 1910, the Journal listed its value at only $40,000.

Excavation began in November 1899. On July 14, 1900, the 10th and Yamhill clubhouse closed with a parade and fireworks celebration. Two days later, the bowling alleys of the new Chapman Street clubhouse opened.

At the September formal opening ball, the public would see Multnomah's new home with its electric lights, indoor track and swimming pool, modern gym and Turkish bath. Social amenities included a dining room, a billiards parlor, a smoking room with a carved stone fireplace mantel, and an extensive member-donated art collection. The cost of the building and its furnishings was deceptively low at $33,200 due to member donations.

The Turkish bath was a fashionable convenience that served MAAC in two ways. First, because members were charged for towels and services, it added to club coffers. More importantly, it contributed to members' health and hygiene – regular bathing was not yet an American custom. Those who soaked, steamed or showered were said to have fewer ailments, a claim MAAC was proud to promote.

Newspaper accounts show that MAAC was undeniably Portland's club and a civic fixture. Club class schedules, events and elections were reported

CHAPTER OPENING PHOTO: Geese roamed the gardens that the Chinese tended at the south end of Multnomah Field. Living in the adjacent shacks, the farmers sold their produce in downtown Portland. Although MAAC had used the athletic field since 1893, it was 1900 before the Chapman Street clubhouse stood to the northeast of these fields. By 1909, the gardens were gone; the club had purchased the site for $60,000. In 1910, the club situated its new clubhouse on Southwest Salmon Street.

The field was a natural amphitheater with Tanner Creek running underground nearby. A lone canoeist takes advantage of flooding in 1904. Throughout the years, the field was raised by adding fill.

The Chapman Street clubhouse opened its doors in July 1900.

and editorialized regularly in all three dailies. Other groups turned to the club for support and cooperation. Board minutes for June 5, 1902, state: "The Portland Rose Club was granted the use of the field for the purpose of holding a rose carnival on two afternoons in June." Thus began a long relationship between MAAC and the Rose Festival.

Women's interest in club membership remained strong. While the Ladies' Annex lacked a separate facility, it still had its own board of directors, classes and public functions. Favored athletic activities included "gymnasium work," swimming, bowling, tennis and basketball.

Showing an enlightened attitude, the club authorized coed sports: bowling and, by 1910, non-competitive swimming. Annex social events were hailed with great anticipation. In 1907, President George McMillan advised

new trustees to take the Ladies' Annex seriously: "Their assistance and membership I feel is absolutely necessary in this club."

PUBLIC BACKS CLUB'S GROWTH

Throughout the decade, Multnomah bore the burden of success. Membership and public interest in club exhibitions continued to strain club facilities. Junior membership closed on more than one occasion. A new classification, intermediate, for young men between 18 and 21, was added. Total membership nearly doubled. When more than 1,000 spectators were turned away from the December 1908 annual Juniors Exhibition, *The Oregonian* and other papers began calling for MAAC's expansion.

In 1909, as it had in 1902, the club mulled the purchase of the Chinese gardens tract south of its field, this time opting to buy at $60,000 "in gold coin of the United States...." At the February general meeting, the membership voted in favor of expansion. That decision, commencing with construction of a new stadium grandstand, was announced on *The Oregonian*'s front page.

The next fall, the renovated facility would accommodate 20,000 school children watching another 3,840 students form a "living" American flag for visiting U.S.

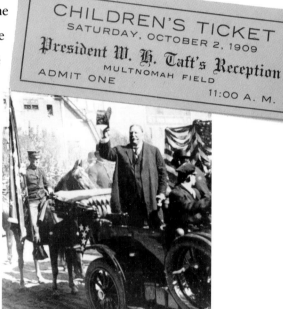

President Taft's 1909 visit to Multnomah Field drew 20,000-plus school children. Robert Krohn, MAAC's athletic instructor, drilled 3,840 students in an exhibition.

President William H. Taft, a sight he described as "the most beautiful and inspiring spectacle I have ever witnessed."

MAAC belonged variously (and sometimes concurrently) to the AAU, the North Pacific Amateur Athletic Association (NPAAA) and the Pacific Northwest Amateur Athletic Association (PNA). The AAU rejected local authorities and records while threatening disbarment of athletes who "professionalized" themselves in non-AAU sanctioned events. (Complaints of professionalism were also regularly and bitterly exchanged by competing clubs that were otherwise friendly.) Frictions were finally resolved when the NPAAA was admitted to the AAU prior to the 1905 Lewis & Clark Exposition Games.

In 1904, Multnomah began a tradition of support for U.S. participation in the Olympics through its contribution of $100 for athletes to attend the St. Louis Games. In 1906, the AAU established the first U.S. Olympic Committee and consequently chose the first sanctioned U.S. team, including MAAC

Fencing was one of many activities available to the members of the Ladies' Annex. Rather than strenuous challenges, the women's exercises stressed grace, poise and form. Robert Krohn is at top, second from right, beside Mrs. Millard C. Holbrook. At far left is Ada Freeman Hoffman.

high-jumper H.W. "Bert" Kerrigan, the first Olympic competitor and medal winner from the West Coast. Four more Multnomah athletes would follow him in the 1908 Games.

KROHN'S ATHLETIC EVENTS INVOLVE THOUSANDS

The rise of sports at large and at MAAC continued throughout the decade. Basketball grew in popularity with the addition of the backboard in mid-decade. Indoor baseball, the forerunner of softball, was an immediate success. "Scientific" boxing and wrestling, as taught by "Professor" J. Fred Rennick and Joe Acton, were popular though still poorly regarded by the non-sporting public.

▶ page 37

T. MORRIS DUNNE

T. Morris Dunne, 21, attended his first MAAC board meeting in 1901 — due to alleged misconduct. Apparently, he was reformed. Later encounters with authority would be as arbiter and leader in a decades-long career in service to MAAC, the AAU and his community.

Though an athlete who was the Lewis & Clark Games' handball champion, Dunne excelled as an administrator. When Seattle interests attempted to monopolize the Pacific Northwest Association of the AAU in 1907, Dunne vigorously protested. Consequently, he was appointed PNA vice president, a position not described in its charter. He later served as its elected secretary and on AAU Olympic selection committees in 1911 and 1923.

An avid golfer, Dunne led the 1916 development of Eastmoreland Golf Course. He was MAAC's first golf committee chairman in 1921.

Between 1904 and 1931, Dunne served 12 years as a trustee, including one year as vice president and two (1930 and 1931) as president.

No single event in Portland history matches the 1905 Lewis & Clark Centennial and American Exposition for sheer impact. Drawing more than three million visitors, it showed Portland to such advantage that the population doubled within five years.

The exposition, held on Northwest Portland wetlands, was organized by city boosters "to celebrate the past and to exploit the future." Timing allowed it to mark the anniversary of the 1805 Lewis & Clark expedition, but its true intent was to attract settlers and investors to the Pacific Northwest. Or, as Col. Henry E. Dosch told The Evening Telegram, "It means money—lots of money."

Asked to direct and control the exposition's amateur sports festival, MAAC hit a snag.

The national offices of the Amateur Athletic Union threatened that the exposition's sports would have to be under AAU control or it would "professionalize all those concerned."

Faced with losing participants, MAAC leader H.W. Kerrigan negotiated to dissolve the North Pacific Amateur Athletic Association and re-form as the Pacific Northwest Association of the AAU. This ensured the games would go on and guaranteed official recognition of Northwest athletes' records.

Kerrigan went on to direct four crowd-pleasing months of competition in events as familiar as baseball, football and gymnastics, and as exotic as fly casting, Indian athletics and auto racing. The drawing power of these contests contributed to the overall success of the exposition, which earned more than $1.5 million for organizers.

White cord marks the lanes in what was probably the 100-yard dash event of the Lewis & Clark Games. MAAC's Forrest Smithson, second from left, finished third to Archie Hahn of the University of Michigan. Parsons of the Olympic Club took first.

A letter to *The Telegram* complained MAAC's boxing matches were "prizefights....The contests were of no value to the community." Member J.N. Teal countered, "The principles of prizefighting are to get your man... by any means. It is not so in boxing. Of course, boxing is not ping-pong. It is a manly game, and it takes men to do it." Nonetheless, women were occasionally permitted to attend matches.

Robert Krohn set the precedent for the next 30 years of physical education at MAAC. A Californian, he was the first West Coast athlete to vault higher than 10 feet. Recruited from the Portland Turn Verein in 1900, he proved to be immensely popular, demonstrating a remarkable talent for remembering names. He initiated gymnasium exercise programs for men and women, including night classes for working men. His synchronized field exhibitions sometimes involved thousands in a single event. In a 1905 MAAC-instituted community program, Krohn launched the Grammar School Athletic League. Ultimately, he left to become physical education director for Portland Public Schools.

Played from the turn of the century through the '20s, indoor baseball included a few interclub competitions. Members of what appears to be a juniors' team include at top, third from left, M.A. Whitehouse; and seated, C. Fischer; Ormandy, the captain; and A.S. Henderson, the pitcher.

MAAC entered the 1910s operating at its athletic and social limits. The Multnomah Boosters Club, formed by long-time members in January 1910, felt that with 2,500 members and 11 acres, a new clubhouse was in order. Expansion fever heated up until the June 16 announcement that the running track in the stadium would be enlarged to meet AAU standards. Unfortunately, that would mean removing the large poplar trees on the south end of the field that were planted when the club first leased it. Sentiment, however, would bow to progress in a loss of this nature.

The MAAC basketball team of 1905, the last club team to play without a backboard. Members were: front, Ed Morris, Dan Bellinger, Art Allen; and back, Harry Fischer, Bert Allen, Robert Krohn, Charles Barton, Vivyan Dent. Krohn introduced the game to the club.

A. C. GILBERT

Olympic hero, train flagman, farm hand, magician, medical student, inventor, wealthy businessman. Alfred Carlton Gilbert lived the life of a child's dreams.

Gilbert's unusual talents were obvious from an early age. As a boy, the Salem native and his friends stole his father's buckboard to put their barn-size "circus" on the road. They were found 60 miles away.

As a young man, Gilbert found international fame as an Olympic champion before opting for medical school at Yale. He paid for his education first by performing as a magician, then by selling kits of his magic tricks. Later, while watching steel bridges from aboard a train, he was inspired to create and patent the Erector Set.

In a 1946 Life magazine article, Gilbert revealed his secret to life and success: having fun.

MAC
CHAMPIONS

The West Coast's first Olympian, *H.W. "Bert" Kerrigan*, held the U.S. high jump record in 1905, when an athlete's feet had to clear the bar first for jumps to be official. Before competing in Athens in 1906, the 5-foot-6-inch Kerrigan had jumped more than 6 feet 2 inches dressed in street clothes, and was said to have made a high jump over a horse.

Kerrigan, favored for the gold, broke some ribs when Mount Vesuvius activity caused a tidal wave that struck his ship. He jumped just 5 feet 8 inches, enough to earn a bronze medal.

In a display of his undiminished prowess, a now-lost photo showed a 65-year-old Kerrigan once again jumping a horse.

Returning from the 1908 London Games, 50 U.S. athletes were feted in a ticker-tape parade past 2.5 million New Yorkers. "Remember boys, you are heroes for 10 days, then go to work," President Teddy Roosevelt advised.

Ten days later, on September 10, MAAC's medalists, Forrest Smithson, Dan J. Kelly and Alfred C. Gilbert, were still celebrating, at the Denver Athletic Club. On September 15, after a torchlight parade past 50,000 cheering Oregonians, the trio received more acclaim at MAAC's lantern-lit field. Accolades were in store the next day at a Commercial Club banquet.

When *Dan Kelly* ran a world record 9.6-second 100-yard dash in July 1905, the AAU at first denied the honor, claiming the time wasn't possible in the "uncivilized Northwest." Charges were even made that timekeepers faked the record.

Sam Bellah

Forrest Smithson

Kelly's silence fueled the controversy, as did his failure to place in the same event at the 1907 AAU national championships.

A U.S. record-holder in the long jump, Kelly won a silver medal in 1908. Later that year he tied the world record in the 220-yard dash, a record held until 1920.

Hurdler *Forrest Smithson* set a world record of 15 seconds to win the gold medal against a field of all-American finalists in the 110-meter event. "I had to make a record to beat that [anti-American] crowd," he proclaimed.

Smithson reputedly never lost a hurdles race until the summer of 1909. Shortly after setting a world record in the 50-meter event in May, he fell in a race at the Armory, losing to fellow MAAC member and future Olympian Martin Hawkins.

When pole vaulter *A.C. Gilbert* surpassed the leader in the London Games by several inches, controversy erupted. Eschewing the standard spike-ended pole, Gilbert had dug a small pit, a vaulting box, in which he planted his pole upon vaulting. London officials allowed him one more try for a tie – but not a victory – if he would use a spiked pole. Gilbert completed the vault with inches to spare, taking a share of the gold. His vaulting box later became the norm.

Pole vaulter *Sam Bellah* finished sixth in the London Games, and seventh in the 1912 Stockholm Olympics. Bellah would later find success as the 1915 AAU national champion.

Bert Kerrigan

Dan J. Kelly

Smithson flies over the hurdles at the 1908 Olympic Games in London. All the finalists in this event were American, while all the officials were British. Disputes over the officiating almost brought the Games to premature closure. Smithson's record-setting victory was so decisive, it was uncontestable by partisan crowds or the officials.

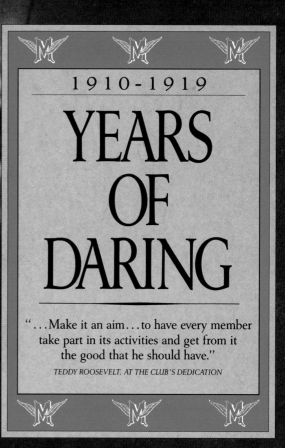

1910-1919

YEARS
OF
DARING

"...Make it an aim...to have every member
take part in its activities and get from it
the good that he should have."

TEDDY ROOSEVELT, AT THE CLUB'S DEDICATION

"Fire!" The silence of the first hour of July 14, 1910, was broken with the cry. The three-story Exposition Building, home to the Fashion Stables, the Nob Hill Kennels, the Brush Automobile Garage and several other businesses, was ablaze. Flames leapt at the building, said to be the largest wooden structure west of the Mississippi and valued at $40,000.

Minutes later, at 12:50 a.m., a general alarm was called. One witness said the fire began inside Dave Honeyman's Apollo Roller Skating Rink, once a Multnomah favorite. Led by Fire Chief David Campbell, a former club boxing instructor, 48 of the city's 50 fire companies reacted, leaving just two on reserve for five other blazes that night.

Fearful of rumors of gasoline drums stored in the Exposition Building's basement, firemen made no attempt to save it, instead turning their efforts to the surrounding area. With the aid of 40 "jackies," barefoot blue-

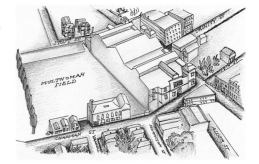

The largest of six fires that evening, the Exposition fire destroyed the area shown in this Oregonian illustration.

jacketed seamen from the visiting gunboat *Yorktown*, the fire was reported under control at 2:30 a.m. The ruins would smolder into the daylight hours.

The final toll was staggering: three deaths, seven city blocks razed, more than a dozen buildings destroyed, at least 20 others damaged, 188 horses and numerous businesses lost, including the Angela Hotel. Damages approached $473,000. The Multnomah Club, at $70,000, was the single biggest loser.

GONE: A PLACE OF CAMARADERIE AND COMPETITION

For club members, the tragedy was especially great. Yes, the records, trophies and works of art were rescued by the valiant efforts of Manager Dow Walker, Swim Coach Arthur Cavill, football player Frank Lonergan, T. Morris Dunne and others. The club strongbox, with all its valuable contents intact, survived the fire — a fact later advertised by its manufacturer.

It was not just that the clubhouse and new steel grandstand were gone: Chapman Street was more than a physical facility. It was a place of camaraderie and competition, a place that lived the ideas and ideals of its day. Suddenly, all that had been reduced to ashes and memories.

CHAPTER OPENING PHOTO: Patrolman William Courtney turned in the first alarm after midnight July 14, 1910. It wasn't long before curtains of flames lit the windows of the Chapman Street clubhouse. MAAC members saved many club artifacts. But the building, along with seven city blocks, was destroyed. Three lives were lost in the neighboring Exposition Building.

The club wasted no time in its response, and community support came quickly. Hours after the fire, in an emergency meeting at the Commercial Club, the board accepted an invitation from the Irvington Tennis Club to use its facility for the July 18 Oregon State Tennis Tournament. A special meeting of "the club, members and the citizens of Portland" was then called. Multnomah would continue despite the odds.

The next evening, President W.A. Holt led the membership in adopting the issuance of $250,000 in secured 20-year bonds to finance the construction of a new clubhouse and stadium. The members rejected a dues increase and delayed opening of bond sales, though by July 31 more than $150,000 worth of bonds had been purchased.

Less than a month after the fire, the old Macleay estate at Southwest Yamhill and Lownsdale (now 15th), leased at $175 a month, was formally opened as temporary quarters. That fall, club members and athletes would use the Vaughn Street baseball grounds for outdoor contests, Ringler's Natatorium for swimming (after briefly using the YMCA and YWCA) and Portland Academy for gymnastics classes.

The old Macleay House (also known as the Kerr House), which stood between Southwest Lownsdale (15th) and 16th at Yamhill and Taylor, was temporary home for MAAC at $175 per month until its Salmon Street clubhouse was ready. Construction of a handball court and purchase of three billiard and pool tables got the nod less than two weeks after the fire.

Looking north from the west side of Multnomah Field the day after the fire, this was the disastrous scene. Heat from the fire was enough to melt the steel girders of the grandstands.

Workmen used jackhammers to free the cornerstone ceremoniously placed by Teddy Roosevelt. Once the marble slab was removed that July day in 1971, the legendary copper box of memorabilia was not to be found.

The Convention Bureau's rival plans for rebuilding the burned area, announced the day after the fire, underscored the civic nature of the Exposition loss. The new million-dollar Greco-Roman design called for an auditorium, stadium, natatorium and replacement Multnomah clubhouse with a separate women's annex. Ultimately, the club's will prevailed without public confrontation.

On November 11, one month after being submitted to building committee chairman George W. Simons, plans for a new clubhouse facing Salmon Street were accepted by the board. Morris Whitehouse, architect and former club baseball star, working fee-free, had rendered 89 pages of blueprints, the basis for creating the finest athletic facility in the American West, estimated to cost $168,000 plus an additional $65,000 or so for furnishings. Its 150,000 square feet would provide "three floors above ground, and basement and subbasement below...44 living rooms, one racquet court, four squash courts and two handball courts, besides a bigger gymnasium than the old one and a swimming tank."

A DEDICATION TOO GOOD TO MISS DRAWS 12,000

Teddy Roosevelt was said to have uttered his famous "Dee-lighted!" when club president Holt invited him to lay the new building's cornerstone. Roosevelt was in the midst of a train excursion through the West at the time, testing the presidential campaign waters. His Portland stop was a mere nine hours long.

Excavation of the Salmon Street hillside had begun only six weeks earlier and the foundation was far from complete, but a presidential dedication was too good to miss.

On April 5, 1911, a day filled with grandstanding and showmanship, an honor guard of Spanish-American War veterans led T.R. to the site. Wielding a specially engraved

Teddy Roosevelt used the specially engraved silver trowel, on the facing page, to spread mortar for laying the cornerstone less than nine months after the Chapman Street clubhouse fire. While the Salmon Street site was far from ready, America's popular ex-president was "dee-lighted" to dedicate it on April 5, 1911. He congratulated club members on their anti-drinking and anti-gambling stands, saying "Drinking tends to tear down the athlete and no one who drinks to excess can have a sound body."

German silver trowel, the ex-president laid the corner-stone of the future clubhouse at what would later be mid-field in the stadium. Nearly all 2,500 club members plus 10,000 others came to watch as T.R. ceremoniously slung mortar. Children sat on fathers' shoulders while others watched from nearby housetops, poles and trees.

"I am particularly pleased that provision is made in the club so that the wives, sisters and daughters of the members should have their share in it too," he intoned. "I haven't much use for the men unless the womenfolk have a part of the fun and I am glad that you take care of the boys and girls. I believe in the sound body and the sound mind...." True to the nature and sentiment of the club's charter, Roosevelt also extolled the virtues of good health, sobriety and avoid-ance of gambling.

The dedication was to have included placing a copper box of mementos inside the cornerstone. For years, everyone believed that it had taken place. Yet, when the clubhouse was razed, no box was found. Sometime after the dedication, Col. A.B. McAlpin described the copper box idea to his son as well-received but not carried out. In the rush of arranging for T.R.'s ceremony no mementos were set aside.

Two short months after the dedication, *The Oregonian* reported that "the finest athletic clubhouse and grounds in the West...[are] being rushed to completion with all possible speed."

The stadium opened June 22 with a club victory in

a baseball game against the University of Keio, Japan, where "Koyama, the Ty Cobb of Mikadoland, proved the real stellar performer of the day...." Then, exactly one year after groundbreaking, the Salmon Street clubhouse opened February 27, 1912. *The Oregonian* listed the building's value at $250,000.

Taking Roosevelt's admonition to heart, the club launched a kaleidoscopic array of programs for all of its members. Activities ranged from chess to water polo. Spring formals, intermediate "hops" and Willamette moonlight dances aboard the *Blue Bird* beckoned the socially minded. The club boasted one of the best libraries in the Pacific Northwest. Dining room service was provided seven days a week by caterer "Professor" James Manley.

To keep members informed, the new *Winged M Bulletin* was launched in November 1913. Unlike its prede-cessor, this publication promised to be a resource, not an irritant.

Participation in Multnomah activ-ities extended deep into the community as well. Multnomah had become the social as well as athletic center for Portland. Club programs and schedules were announced in newspaper features; patronesses of MAAC dances had their portraits printed on the society page; and ladies' and juniors' exhibitions con-tinued to be favored by performers and spec-tators alike.

Multnomah's reach was best demonstrated in the combined dedication of the Columbia River Highway and opening day of the seventh annual Rose Festival May 17, 1913, at Multnomah Field. A Robert

▶ *page 48*

When The Oregonian *reported on the Multnomah Club's July 1908 Low Jinks expedition to the Columbia Slough, the story chronicled what seemed like a pleasant and jovial all-male outing—a lively river cruise of nearly 250 men on the T. J. Neal, with friendly dousings, swimming, good food, plenty of baseball, football, running, boxing and wrestling, and music by the Parsons Orchestra—a real boys-will-be-boys adventure. About the only hint of anything unusual is the mention that "everybody got home safe and sound, although some were minus a little clothing."*

The club's August 25 board minutes tell a somewhat different story.

"Indecent-

The Undine, *like the* Beaver, the Madeline, *and other steamships, carried MAAC men to Low Jinks, a day of unabandoned fun. Perhaps in response to the rowdiness, later outings included a club patrol wagon. Organized games, like this large push ball, created large appetites.*

low-jinks-pictures committee reports suppression of offensive prints," it reads. And in October, the minutes mention the board has settled a "low jinks damage case" and appropriated $100 for legal services.

Exactly what happened during the 1908 outing was not recorded in club histories, but whatever it was, it ended "Low Jinks" for six years. And, while attempts were made to revive the tradition between 1914 and 1923, the growing wildness and rowdiness that had peaked in 1908 effectively killed this rite of summer.

The idea for Low Jinks began innocently enough in June 1896, when some 80 members of the club's cycling group, the Multnomah Wheelmen, set out for a cross-country bicycle ride and picnic. The Oregonian reported that the Wheelmen went to Stansbury Grove, near Columbia Slough, "on their wheels, a well-loaded wagon in charge of L. J. Goldsmith having preceded them, and put in a day that each and every one described as one of 'unalloyed joy and bliss.' There was plenty to eat, and cool, refreshing Bull Run to drink. A highly exciting baseball game was played, and after the game everyone who could went swimming. Those who couldn't swim ventured themselves on treacherous rafts that meanly betrayed the trust reposed in them.''

The paper also remarked that some participants were observed afterward limping about the clubhouse.

Although the men used bicycles that first year, as the outing grew the tradition developed of taking railcars, small boats or steamboats to various spots along the Columbia and Lewis rivers. Each year, there was an abundance of food, fun, games, music — and a little more rowdiness, until the debacle of 1908.

After six years of cooling off, Low Jinks returned in 1914 and 1915, but by 1916 club members decided to hold a ''High Jinks'' instead — a family picnic at Crystal Lake Park. The idea took hold, but the event itself was soon renamed the Annual Picnic, which continued until 1928.

Low Jinks was revived again in 1921 and 1922, but in 1923 had to be called off twice because of weather. This, plus pressure from the board, spelled the end. The Winged M Bulletin of June 27, 1924 includes a lament for Low Jinks by the anonymous ''Gahoozla Bird,'' who wrote, ''Gone are the days of 'shirts off,' gone are the days of the old barn and its secrets, gone are the days of blistered backs, gone are the days of the mud cannibals, gone are the days of the whirling cakes of ice, and gone are the days when men members of the club took a day off, forgot their dignity and became boys again. 'Tis too bad, we admit, but truly 'them days is gone forever.' ''

THIS SILK RACING SINGLET WAS FOUND IN
A HOUSE IN ASTORIA OWNED BY THE
TALLANT FAMILY. TRACK STAR WILLIAM
TALLANT SET THE PACIFIC NORTHWEST
AMATEUR ATHLETIC ASSOCIATION MILE
RECORD IN 1895. HE TRAINED BY RUNNING
THE HILLS OF ASTORIA, ACCORDING TO
FRANK WATKINS' HISTORICAL ACCOUNT.
"WHEN HE PUT ON SPIKED SHOES AND
GOT ON A LEVEL TRACK, IT WAS SO EASY
FOR HIM THAT HE COULD NOT HELP
WINNING THE RACE BY ABOUT A
LAP," WATKINS WROTE IN
THE WINGED M BULLETIN.

Krohn extravaganza featured 6,500 Portland school children in a variety of events, including one calisthenics demonstration in which 3,000 pupils took part.

The spirit of temperance pervaded American life, culminating in passage of the 18th Amendment to the U.S. Constitution by 1920. Alcohol was already forbidden in the clubhouse. Other moderating values filtered into club life, and Physical Director "Professor" Otto C. Mauthe exemplified those notions best.

COMMUNITY EXTRAVAGANZAS DISPLAY PHYSICAL PROWESS

The multifaceted Mauthe came to the club with an obscure and intriguing past. An 1895 graduate of Indiana Normal School, he was reputed to have taught at Harvard and schools in Illinois, Louisiana, California and elsewhere. *The Portland Telegram* curiously, and without elaboration, credited him with "international fame as the originator of patrol drills." Regardless, his prodigious talent for producing such spectacular exhibitions routinely packed the stadium.

Shortly after his arrival in 1916, Mauthe organized Multnomah High Jinx, a summer family picnic at Crystal Lake Park in Milwaukie, staged in stark contrast to the rowdy all-male Low Jinx. His exercise classes for men, women and children stressed discipline and character. Those displaying such virtues were awarded "Leader" status and entitled to wear a large "L" on their blouse, singlet or shirt.

Mauthe had many of the same personable traits that made predecessor Robert Krohn such an endearing figure to the club. He earned the marvel and appreciation of class members for giving each member individual attention at some point during classes. He was said to be able to dance with every student in his ladies' classes during the instructional period. When prodded with the question about what would happen if his classes grew to 200 or more, he responded that the club would

O.C. Mauthe, endearingly called "Professor," was dedicated to youth and family programs. At MAAC from 1916 until 1927, he directed the club's annual Spring Exhibitions and other well-attended extravaganzas. He taught at Oregon Agricultural College, later Oregon State College, until his 1939 death.

The practice of naming "Leaders" in large athletic drill classes was instituted by O.C. Mauthe. Those who earned the title wore it or the letter "L" on their shirts. Youth were so important to Mauthe, he established Camp Olympus, a summer camp for boys and girls, at Summit Lake near Olympia, Washington.

have to find larger facilities, never giving thought or credence to diminishing his personal attention.

After an 11-year tenure, Mauthe left MAAC for a position at Oregon Agricultural College.

CLAMORING TO COMPETE IN CRIMSON AND WHITE

Despite the Exposition fire, Multnomah athletes stormed through the decade with unabated enthusiasm. The Winged M football squad, an early Northwest version of "America's Team," was the team that fans — and players — loved to love or to hate. The team dominated play on the West Coast, at one point racking up three consecutive unbeaten seasons. Collegiate stars throughout the nation sought the chance to wear the crimson and white.

EDGAR E. FRANK

A member of one of Portland's most prominent merchant families, wrestler Edgar E. Frank's combative, competitive attitude belied his patrician upbringing. A junior member in 1892, Frank was described as "a slight little chap with nothing but athletic ambition and bulldog pluck."

A scant 90-pounder in 1900, he won the first boxing and wrestling meets he entered, despite competing in the 115-pound class. At the 1905 Lewis & Clark Games, Frank won the West Coast wrestling championship, a title he retained through 1911. Frank took second place at the 1907 national AAU meet in Newark, and a first in the 1909 all-Western tournament in Chicago.

As a committee man, Frank started "smokers" — interclub boxing and wrestling matches — in 1905. In 1907, at 22, he became the youngest MAAC board member ever, serving until 1915, and was vice president in 1910. In 1908, he created the intermediate membership category. Frank was twice head of the Pacific Northwest AAU. In recognition, he received a MAAC honorary membership in 1909. *(continued)*

FRANK cont'd.

In 1911, after a four-year effort, Frank succeeded in having the club host the national AAU wrestling meet at the Heilig Theatre.

The tragedy of Frank's untimely death was matched only by the drama surrounding it. In March 1917, while promoting another MAAC-hosted national meet, he was hospitalized in Chicago with blood poisoning. When he did not respond to a MAAC telegram, his mother and brother began a race with death to be with him.

Frank lived just long enough for his mother to arrive at his bedside. MAAC cancelled all upcoming social and athletic events, including the national wrestling match he championed.

Wrestling flourished at MAAC under the tutelage of Edward J. O'Connell, Yale's first wrestling coach and 1908 Olympic coach. O'Connell met Edgar Frank at the national wrestling championships in Newark in 1907 and defected to the club in September 1908, lured by the offer of $750 for 10 months' services. The club's national reputation was established when it hosted the 1911 AAU championships and produced a local champion. During O'Connell's 11-year tenure, this world champion welterweight developed a stable of wrestlers who would go on to win several national championships, plus two gold medals and one silver in the 1924 Olympics.

With the development of overhand shooting styles, club basketball finally came into its own in mid-decade. In true MAAC fashion, the team mastered its foes on a regular basis. Still, basketball remained a curiously glamourless enterprise. As soon as the football season ceased, MAAC basketball teams earned their column inches in the dailies. But the sport never gained the idolizing respect football received, and no "name" players emerged.

Basketball was one of the few competitive sports deemed suitable for ladies. Their games, with combined team scores in the teens, must have made the men's seem supersonically fast — men's game totals approached 40 points.

When ice hockey first made its presence known in Portland in 1914 through the work of member W. A. Kearns, Multnomah again moved to the fore. In mid-October, 150 skaters and enthusiasts joined a Kearns-led meeting at the newly constructed Ice Hippodrome (later known as the Ice Palace) at Northwest 25th and Marshall to create the Portland Amateur Hockey Asso-

▶ *page 52*

Hockey came to Portland in 1914 with MAAC's assistance. Interrupted by WWI, the hockey era ended in 1930 but not without the MAAC team of Bennett, Watt, Jackson, Alexander, Sandberg, Hamilton, Dallas, Rabideau, Ritz, Edge, Markett and Des Brisay tying with Seattle for the Pacific Northwest championship.

Multnomah members were clearly not content to confine their diversions to the clubhouse. Mountain adventures and winter forays to the beach were part of the club itinerary, as were swimming excursions to Ross Island, where members traveled by skiff to the floating Windemuthe Baths for a dip in the Willamette.

On July 1, 1916, an expeditionary group of Multnomah and Mazama hikers traveled via train and then auto through White Salmon, Washington, and after a rendezvous with "a detachment of four automobiles," hiked to timberline to attempt a July 4 assault on Mount Adams. On July 5, The Telegram reported that MAAC climbers Nelson English and H.L. Wilbur "managed to reach the summit of Mount Adams, out of the 68 starting....The two men were forced to crawl on their hands and knees for the last few hundred feet owing to the terrific force of the wind, which at the same time drove small particles of glass-like snow and ice into their faces. The party encountered snow five miles lower down than usual at this time of the year."

Yet, not all of the extracurricular adventures were athletic ones. Promoted by the Women's Annex and led by swimming enthusiast Arthur "Tums" Cavill, mid-winter assaults on the beaches at Gearhart drew as many as 230 club members at a time. Such weekend excursions were an annual feature during Tums' tenure at the club. Chartered trains took members to the Hotel Gearhart for beach bonfires and midnight splashes in the surf, followed by dancing until 3 a.m. The frivolities came to an end soon after Cavill left in 1913 for Seattle. It is unclear whether the end of the beach excursions was due to the loss of Tums' leadership. Club records hint the Hotel Gearhart may have pulled up its welcome mat.

Arthur "Tums" Cavill, in the surf at center, was a thrill-seeking Australian who was persuaded to come to MAAC on June 4, 1909. This 1912 Gearhart dip, like the Christmas Day swims, was a Cavill-promoted idea. He died of hypothermia in 1913 from attempting to swim Seattle's Elliot Bay.

From 1910 to 1913, more than 200 MAAC members would make the Hotel Gearhart their weekend getaway. Forming a human chain, they march lockstep to the dining room.

MAC

Martin W. Hawkins

George Philbrook

Four club athletes competed in the 1912 Stockholm Olympics: *Walter McClure* in the mile run; *George Philbrook* in the shot, discus and pentathlon; *Sam Bellah*, in his second Olympic pole vault competition; and *Martin Hawkins* in the 110-meter hurdles. Hawkins was the only one to win a medal, a bronze.

Before 1909, Hawkins was a less-than-successful sprinter for the University of Oregon and the Multnomah Club. When returning MAAC Olympic athletes headlined a track meet at the Oregon National Guard Armory, Hawkins opted at the last minute to compete in his first-ever 50-yard hurdles. When race leader and undefeated world record-holder Forrest Smithson fell, Hawkins surged to victory. Thus Hawkins' first hurdles race and victory came in Smithson's first hurdles loss. Hawkins then went on to win every high hurdles competition until one in which he, too, fell.

Philbrook was a 1908 PNA record-holder in the discus. A football tackle and line coach for Notre Dame, he later served as a club track team manager in 1917 and coach in 1919. He placed fifth in shot and seventh in discus in Stockholm. Competing in the 1912 pentathlon against legendary athlete Jim Thorpe and others, he apparently injured himself when his vaulting pole snapped. Some said had he not withdrawn, Philbrook would have had enough points for the bronze.

Walter Hummell, the first MAAC athlete to be named All-American since Kelly, Smithson and Gilbert, streaked to national prominence in September 1916. A 440-yard hurdler, Hummell was captain of the MAAC track and field team. He set a national record at the AAU junior championship in Newark and followed that with a meet record and the senior championship the next day. Hummell was quickly named to the All-American track and field team. He died in World War I.

As a junior member and Washington High School senior in 1912, Vere Windnagle set a national record in the half-mile that stood as the Oregon high school record for 50 years. In 1914 at Cornell, he ran the mile in 4:15, just 4/10ths of a second off the world record. Windnagle then broke the world record in the 880 only to see it snatched away later in the same meet. In 1917 he joined the ranks of All-Americans in track and field.

Norman Ross

Flamboyant *Norman Ross*, a Jack Cody-trained swimmer who won the 1912 Christmas swim and the 1914 Willamette River Marathon, racked up PNA, national and world championships and records. Just two days out of a St. Johns smallpox "pest-house," he gained international recognition for his victories at the 1915 Panama-Pacific International Exposition. His career culminated with gold medals in the 400-meter freestyle, the 1500-meter freestyle and the 4 x 200-meter relay at the 1920 Antwerp Olympics. Though still a MAAC member, Ross competed wearing Illinois Athletic Club colors. Following the Olympics, a honeymooning Ross visited MAAC with his Hawaiian bride before returning to Chicago and a career as a radio personality.

In boxing and wrestling, *Oscar Franzke* compiled a decade-long record that culminated in his national AAU wrestling championship in front of a home audience at the Heilig Theatre (now the Fox) in May 1911.

The year 1915 brought weightlifting fame to MAAC with the efforts of *Al Tauscher* and *Owen Carr*, the first two Americans to break world records. At a time when the sport was thought to be a health hazard (although cigarettes were not), the 5-foot-4-inch, 150-pound Tauscher was first to lift more than twice his body weight in the two-arm jerk and to lift two pounds more than his own weight in the one-arm snatch. At 162 pounds in 1916, Tauscher set another record of 210 pounds in the one-arm jerk. His amazing abilities in various athletics led to seven decades as a MAAC instructor.

In the first West Coast amateur weightlifting meet at San Francisco, Carr, a mere 158 pounds, took second place to a 215-pound rival. At 165 pounds, he set an unofficial world record in the wrestler's bridge, hoisting 310 pounds. He had a long career as an instructor with both the Portland Public Schools and the club.

Owen Carr

Al Tauscher with an artillery shell in a Marine Corps display at Quantico, Virginia.

57

The 1913 arrival of Coach Jack Cody, "world champion diver," rang in MAAC's era of the diver. By 1918 the club was amassing state, regional and national championships, including those from MAAC-hosted nationals that year. The climax came in 1920 when Louis "Happy" Kuehn and Thelma Payne won Olympic medals.

Women now showed their abilities in the first competitive sport deemed acceptable for them. Aided by new, less restrictive (and slightly scandalous) swimsuits with open neck and arm holes, women quickly grabbed the opportunity to show their athletic talents. MAAC women soon proved themselves to be among the most able divers anywhere.

Constance Meyer

Helen Hicks, Louis "Happy" Kuehn and Jack Cody.

Mrs. Constance Meyer — contemporary news accounts always included the title — was clearly a modern woman. A divorcee with "the nerve of a bank robber," she claimed she learned to swim in her early 20s after falling from her horse — in the middle of the Columbia River. Meyer took up competitive diving in her mid-30s and was the club's first woman to forcefully spring rather than daintily step from the end of the board. She earned her first championship at the 1916 Panama-Pacific International Exposition, then two years later placed third in the AAU national championships. Selected for the 1920 Olympic team, Meyer made the long journey only to find she would be treated as an alternate in Antwerp and not be allowed to compete, a fact she decried bitterly. Teams had been told to bring six competitors for each event, though only four were needed.

The 1918 AAU championships displayed homegrown club talent. *Helen Hicks* placed second; she later won the the 1920 Oregon and the 1921 PNA championships. *Virginia Pembrooke*, whose sister *Irene Pembrooke* was also a popular exhibition diver, placed third three consecutive years (1919-1921) in the PNA championships.

The crowning glory of 1918 was *Thelma Payne's* first of three consecutive national titles, a feat no woman has since duplicated. Her victory gave

MAAC a sweep in the women's division. When Payne, the city hall switchboard operator, was tapped for the 1920 Olympics, the city council granted her a two-month paid leave of absence. Perhaps the toughest challenge was a nightmarish trans-Atlantic voyage replete with crowded below-deck accommodations, spoiled food and a near-mutiny by athletes. Despite a foot injury and apparent biased officiating at the Games, Payne won the bronze medal in the three-meter springboard event. She considered this a poor showing as she had defeated the gold and silver medalists in other competitions.

Louis Balbach's career began at the club in 1913 and led to the 1920 Olympics. He placed first in the 10-meter dive at the 1916 Panama-Pacific International Exposition, second at the 1916 AAU nationals, and first in the 1918 state championships. Though still a club member, Balbach competed in the 1920 Antwerp Games courtesy of his alma mater, Columbia University, whose colors he wore. (At the time, there were no U.S. team uniforms.) The Cody-trained diver won the bronze medal in three-meter springboard diving and placed sixth in 10-meter platform competition.

Louis "Happy" Kuehn was a two-time state diving champion and, at 19, the 1919 national junior diving champion on the three-meter springboard. In Antwerp, Kuehn became the first American to win the gold medal in Olympic diving. After his competitive career ended, he remained active on MAAC committees for many years.

Through the 1920s, other divers achieved regional and national distinction, among them *George Richardson*, a junior member and "the club's tiniest diver"; *Gladys Stansbury*, who took first in the 1923 PNA championships; and *Lillian Knutsen*, who won the Oregon junior championship in 1926 and the national junior championship in 1927. Multnomah never attained such diving prominence again.

Lillian Knutsen

Thelma Payne

1920-1929

THE CIVIC CLUB

"Make big plans; aim high in hope and work, remembering that a noble logical diagram once recorded will not die."

DANIEL H. BURNHAM

Multnomah had truly come of age. The club's blend of sport, high society and civic involvement mirrored Portland's post-war affluence. MAAC entered the decade maintaining itself on dues alone, as it had for a few years. It could afford to strut in public, and Portland responded with eager approval.

As a meeting ground for the socially and civically prominent, MAAC was seen by local newspapers as both an initiator and a barometer of public affairs — what was good for the club was good for Portland, and vice versa. The club provided the city with teams and athletes to root for as well as an untainted venue for competitions. Portland also increasingly found need to use Multnomah Field for civic purposes, and it was willingly offered.

The Oregonian, *The Telegram*, and the *Oregon Journal* carried announcements of the club's activities in earlier years, but their coverage in the 1920s reached an unparalleled scale. Photos of club-event patronesses increased in size and number in the society pages. Club exhibitions and performances received weeks of advance notice. Editorials commented on club activities and policies as if to affect their outcome.

COMMUNITY NEED FUELS STADIUM EXPANSION

Private rumblings for a new civic stadium went public in L.H. Gregory's 1921 *Oregonian* sports column: "[It's] time to point out that Portland…has no big athletic and community stadium built or under way." The former *Winged M Bulletin* editor suggested that MAAC assume that responsibility.

The need certainly appeared to be there. Football's popularity had reached new heights. The Rose Festival's Rosaria Pageant caused the stands to overflow. When U.S. President Warren Harding visited in 1923, "They filled the seats to capacity and overflowed into the field….They perched themselves high in the windows of the club….They sat upon the grass…and some venturesome ones climbed telephone poles." *The Oregonian* estimated the crowd at 25,000-30,000.

Grandstand enlargements in 1923 doubled stadium capacity to 15,000, making news from Walla Walla to Astoria. Yet the stadium's major tenants — the University of Oregon, Oregon Agricultural College and the Rose Festival Association — pressed for even better, still larger facilities. (In fact, college football had outdrawn club gridiron contests since 1915.) MAAC could not ignore

CHAPTER OPENING PHOTO: *After a week of headlines anticipating their arrival, the U.S. Navy Pacific Fleet football team and 100-piece marching band sailed in with a convoy of destroyers for the final game of the 1920 season. The Oregonian reported, ''Multnomah might have had a chance if it had been allowed to mine the field, but that is one of the few things barred from football.'' The final score was 41-0.*

public sentiment. President John A. Laing told members the club bore "the immediate responsibility of developing its field to put Portland on the map for football, the Rose Festival and the other full-sized activities for our growing metropolis."

At the 1925 annual meeting, members gave their enthusiastic approval to a new $500,000 Multnomah Civic Stadium seating 28,000. A stadium association was formed in late February, with committees representing community interests from Portland Public Schools to the Boy Scouts.

In March, a novel plan to underwrite construction costs was devised. It called for community groups to sell $100 "plaques" that gave buyers free seats for five years and reserved those seats for five more years.

A.E. Doyle's original plans for the stadium called for a larger facility than today's, but the club did not own all the land along 18th Avenue. Thus, the east grandstand was never built.

Sales began in early March; by May 14, $300,000 had been raised, enough to begin construction. One week earlier, MAAC members optimistically approved the issue of $550,000 in gold bonds secured by club holdings appraised at $1.7 million. The bonded debt would be sufficient to complete the stadium and refund the club's unmatured debts.

Alumni from the University of Oregon and Oregon Agricultural College were among many community groups that set out to sell stadium plaques to fund expansion of the facility. In less than two and a half months, $300,000 had been raised.

MAC
MEMORABILIA

The November 3, 1922, Winged M Bulletin reported that OAC's Beavers "had the same trouble year after year. In spots they appear as champions. Then they falter...nothing is more uncertain in life than an OAC football team." When the unbeaten-though-injury-weakened MAAC squad faced the winless Beavers, they were surprised with "the tightest game seen on the local field this season." A late-game touchdown kept MAAC's streak intact.

The football itself was a far cry from its blunt-ended forebear. The threat of the dropkick was on the decline; the forward pass now ruled and needed a projectile whose shape lent itself more to the hand rather than the toe. But as tradition still dictates, the game winner kept the ball.

MAAC Football Yields to Collegiate Contests

On October 9, 1926, Multnomah Civic Stadium was formally dedicated. One week later, the MAAC football team played its last game, ending a 35-year history. Football had once been Multnomah's reason for being and Multnomah championed its cause throughout the Northwest. Now, ironically, because of that advocacy, amateur football had given way to domination by college teams. The stadium built by club football would never be home to a MAAC team.

The club, one 1923 *Oregonian* editor opined, had "but a small fraction of the members that an institution of its character, purpose and service should have."

Apparently MAAC trustees agreed. Despite the fact that club facilities were often strained to capacity, membership drives became an annual occurrence. Membership was constantly in a state of flux. In 1919, there were nearly 5,500 members; in 1927, 4,900. Guest nights, two-week visitors' passes and discounted initiation fees enticed prospective members. Potential problems with excessive growth were greeted with optimistic talk of further expansion.

While America wrestled with Prohibition, Multnomah proudly basked in the calm of its own temperance. At no other time since its inception would the club so proudly testify to its sobriety.

U.S. President Warren G. Harding spoke at the stadium in 1923.

That and the club ban on gambling meant "No scandal has ever besmirched the fair name of Multnomah," 1920 President C. Henri Labbe observed. Still, to be a club member did not mean to want for entertainment.

As the decade advanced, MAAC reached for an unequaled level of social sophistication. Its first dinner dance, in 1922, was called a "marked success" as were moonlight cruises, ladies' nights, costume balls, and Saturday night dances with Olsen's Orchestra. Club exhibitions, including the 1927 Society Circus, attracted 5,000 or more spectators. By 1929, the KGW Quartet performed dance selections in live remote broadcasts from the club.

SPECTATORS, RECREATION PUT NEW ANGLE ON SPORTS

"The growth of recreational sports in the last dozen years has come from a realization that work should be supplemented by play," *The Oregonian* told its readers in 1925. While MAAC still had its competitive teams and athletes, the emphasis for many members was on play. Recreational sports, undertaken for the simple pleasure of participation, captured the club's collective spirit.

Club officials greet "Gentleman" Jim Corbett, first world heavyweight boxing champion under the Marquis of Queensbury rules. "Why, the businessmen of Portland don't know what they have here," Corbett declared. "There isn't another club in the world that has grounds like those."

Members took up golf, racquet and other court sports. Squash was discovered by a large following and two new courts were added to the existing pair. Tennis courts increased, too, to seven. Volleyball gained respectability. Baseball was revitalized in the intramural "Sunday Morning League" and the re-formed interclub team.

The spectator's role assumed even greater importance. With more choices than ever, the fans determined the distinction between serious and recreational athletics and the success of sports like football and hockey. Sports were now more dependent upon spectators for sheer viability.

Tennis, more than any other sport, typified the '20s at MAAC. The game had been played locally for 30 years. Since 1899, MAAC had hosted the state championships, producing its share of winners including nationally acclaimed Phil Neer and perennial city and state contender Jack Rhine. In the '20s, though, tennis also gained the trappings of status.

The 1921 Oregon State Tennis Tournament was the quintessence of society sport. *The Oregonian* reported, "The courts and the tea booth are centers of interest. Maids and matrons in smart summery frocks and sport togs are to be seen each afternoon enjoying the social side of the event, as well as the fine plays of the participants. . . .The tennis dance will be the event of note for this evening."

LURE OF THE LINKS EVENTUALLY TRAPS MAAC

Golf had been played in the United States for 33 years, and in Portland for a quarter century when MAAC finally decided it should stage its own

▶ *page 68*

THE GROO-PELOUZE ROMANCE

MAAC members were known for winning in heated competition. Bobby Pelouze, a bond salesman, MAAC football captain and ex-Stanford football star, claimed victory in one of the keenest rivalries of the 1920s — for the hand of Miss Julia S. Groo.

Winner of a fully furnished $15,000 electrical dream home in an electric utility's 1925 essay contest, Miss Groo quickly received many proposals of marriage. Pelouze and a teammate appeared on her Sellwood district doorstep, MAAC football in hand, and asked her to inscribe it for Multnomah luck in an upcoming match. Pelouze then returned to the city and said, "Miss Groo has had 400 proposals of marriage — and mine will be 401."

His was the one she accepted, and the couple wed in 1926.

For two-plus decades, the Winged M was the Northwest's football team. Its victories were Portland's pride; shameful losses seldom made headlines. MAAC's undefeated seasons and lopsided scores were reported from Ketchikan to Phoenix. Players from Notre Dame, Stanford, Michigan and Penn State made MAAC their second alma mater.

The 1906 introduction of the sidearm-slung forward pass led football away from reliance on mass, but Multnomah resisted change. Player Gordon Moores complained the new rules ''completely revolutionize the game and extract from it many of the spectacular features that make it our great winter sport.'' MAAC's slow, soggy barkdust turf favored bulk and brawn. Yet the University of Oregon used speed to defeat MAAC in 1906 for the first time in their 10-year-old rivalry.

Despite the addition of helmets and pads, from 1905 to 1910 football brutality took a nationwide toll of 113 deaths and nearly 800 major injuries. Safety improved only when playing styles evolved to counter Notre Dame's astonishing 1913 success with the forward pass.

Amateurism existed in appearance only. Under AAU rules, a paid coach could play for his team. Foes accused MAAC teams of putting 12 ''coaches'' in the lineup. And, players were recruited with jobs at club-members' firms. To maintain the facade of amateurism, in accordance with the rules, Sunday games were prohibited.

The Multnomah-Olympic Club rivalry resumed in 1915 and was cloaked in controversy. Dudley Clarke's alleged professional play in 1913 led to a brouhaha exploited in

Despite the presence of Stanford all-star Bobby Pelouze and other former college greats, the 1926 Winged M team was held scoreless and gave up 122 points in its two-game final season. The last MAAC squad is pictured here.

both cities' newspapers. MAAC's Clarke defused the incident by leaving football for Hollywood Westerns, and the game ended in a scoreless tie as had the last match in 1899. Featuring the Notre Dame-style "rejuvenated football" with overhand spiral passes, it drew raves nonetheless.

Both World War I and the NCAA four-year rule appeared in 1917, limiting the careers of college players. Former soldiers who had waged war on Sundays were willing to play on the day amateur athletes could not. Their ardor and strategic approach to the collegiate game heralded the arrival of legitimate professional football and the impending demise of club teams.

Members of the Winged M squad including Chuck Rose, left; and Hale, second from right; on the bench circa 1923.

The birth of the Pacific Coast Conference further eroded MAAC football. Subject to NCAA rules, these teams avoided "professionals." And by the '20s, with full-time coaches, college standards had risen dramatically.

Despite a disappointing 1925 season, President John Laing augured, "We are confident of the permanency of football as a club sport." Construction of the new $500,000 stadium proceeded as planned.

The 1926 season opened; Multnomah still faltered. Key players missed practice. The once-touted field remained an uninviting bog.

After a 67-0 opening loss to Oregon Agricultural College, MAAC revamped its lineup. The next Saturday, October 16, groundskeepers worked feverishly to drain the rain-soaked field for a game with "the Notre Dame of the West," Gonzaga College of Spokane.

All was to no avail. Mudbath and bloodbath, the Bulldogs shredded the Winged M, 55-0.

Club trustees quickly took stock. MAAC games had few spectators. Colleges practiced as much in a day as Multnomah did in a week. Professional teams lured players with big crowds and big money. MAAC and the Olympic Club were the only club teams left in the nation. It would be pointless to continue. The once-mighty team disbanded immediately.

Less than a week after that final loss, MAAC's new civic stadium was officially dedicated.

The team's final fall from grace obscured its glorious past — a 35-year legacy of 138 wins, 58 losses and 22 ties.

An unsuccessful attempt led by Frank Watkins to form a team in 1928 forced the inescapable conclusion: The game that made Multnomah was no longer Multnomah's game.

Former U of O football great Cedric "Hap" Miller, left, coached MAAC's team while working as an attorney in Vancouver. Harry Fischer, right, was team manager for two years. Joining the club about 1902, Fischer played some football and a lot of basketball when young. Fischer, a committee member on numerous occasions, lived at MAAC for many years.

THE BASEBALL TOUR OF 1929

Asked by Australian sports federations to bring an exceptional American amateur baseball team "down under," the Matson Steamship Co. invited MAAC to send its best. So, like missionaries, 12 Multnomah men set out in July 1929 to spread the word on baseball throughout the South Pacific.

The youngest player on the nearly three-month trip was 15-year-old Bob Grayson, who joined his brother Buck, along with Harry Dillon, George Story, Brian Mimnaugh, Vincent Jacobberger, Ralph Davis, Hugh "Dinty" Moore, Kenneth Sax, Fred Helmcke, Sharkey Sherritt and Bill Smyth. All had played on club teams for at least two years.

Though MAAC lost four matches in Hawaii, its Australian record was a stunning 11 wins, one tie, no losses before a total audience of 100,000. One news writer called MAAC the "greatest amateur team ever to show

(continued)

tournaments. After the war, golf became a national rage, so MAAC formed its first golf committee in 1921. Trend-setting members of MAAC and three other local clubs underwrote the 1916 construction of the Eastmoreland Golf Course on land donated by the Ladd family. Led by T. Morris Dunne and Parks Superintendent J.O. "Dad" Conville, a longtime MAAC football stalwart, Eastmoreland was created through a temporary private and public partnership. City ownership began with the first nine holes in 1923.

That August, threatened with the erosion of its membership to private golf clubs, MAAC began searching for its own golf course site. As *The Oregonian's* L.H. Gregory said, "Golf is no longer a luxury for an athletic club — it's a necessity — and parking places for golf-panted athletes must be provided in every up-to-date lobby...."

In March 1924, a Raleigh Hills site off Canyon Road was chosen over 16 others, and soon after, the Multnomah Golf Club, "a distinct and separate corporation," was formed. The club launched a campaign to subscribe 500 men and women at $300 each. More than 130 signed up within two hours of the opening sale. A year later, MAAC's 18-hole, 6,690-yard championship links, designed by San Francisco architect Willie Lock, opened with A.B. McAlpin as manager.

"Terrible Ted" Thye

After the 1920 Olympics, competitive diving lost some of its luster. Wrestling soon filled the void as the club's preeminent competitive sport. Coach and professional light heavyweight world champion wrestler Ted Thye capitalized on the work of predecessor Ed O'Connell, producing Olympians and national champions throughout the decade. Thye's professional career prospered too. Though he lost his title during a 1925 Australian tour, Thye still retained the nickname "Terrible Ted" at the end of the decade.

Boxers under the tutelage of Tom Louttit pounded out their glory as the sport recovered from a widespread scandal of the late Teens.

Professional boxing was illegal in Oregon, but amateur clubs could keep gate receipts from scheduled bouts. Unscrupulous promoters sometimes formed sham clubs with only a solitary member until a Frank Watkins-led commission restored order.

In May 1921, *The Oregonian* reported: "Inter-club boxing smokers of the kind held at the Multnomah amateur club Tuesday night...are a fine thing for amateur boxing, the revival of which hereabouts is coming along lustily." By the end of the decade, sports-page headlines referred to amateur boxers and wrestlers as simon-pures.

Though Multnomah sent fewer athletes to the Olympics than in the previous decade, its support remained undiminished. In 1925, the member-

Although men played in full-length pants, female tennis players faced a greater challenge taking to the courts in ankle-length dresses and petticoats. Despite the clothing restrictions, the popularity of tennis continued to grow throughout the 20th century.

ship approved the "Watkins amendment" to the club charter, assessing each member for a donation to the U.S. Olympic fund.

The '20s ended with national economic turmoil. Despite efforts to maintain appearances, MAAC was no exception. Civic stadium, once Multnomah's pendant gem, quickly became its financial albatross. The club's new manager, James J. Richardson, was admired for his promotional skills, but the adversity of the Depression years would call for much resourcefulness and ingenuity. "Multnomah spirit" would soon have new connotations.

BASEBALL TOUR cont'd.

in the islands," comparing it to a "mediocre" Stanford team that had visited earlier. Another account called their play "a revelation....The most spectacular part... has been their hitting power, the like of which has never been seen in Australia."

These smashing victories didn't dampen the team's reception. Hospitality was unabashedly enthusiastic. The men, eager to please their hosts, even played in a downpour rather than disappoint spectators. As Smyth wrote in a letter home, "...each man is doing all he can to further the name of the club." In that they did succeed, and the entire city of Portland showed its appreciation with a gala banquet featuring speeches by the mayor and other city officials.

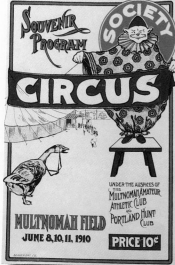

It grew to be a rite of spring, along with the rhododendrons and the rain: Multnomah men, women and children parading in colorful costumes, performing their athletic, gymnastic and "aesthetic" specialties for an audience of thousands. It was the spring exhibition, Multnomah's ode to physical culture, and it was popular in one form or another during MAAC's first 40 years.

Starting with "parents' nights" in the 1890s, members could witness the gymnastic progress made by their children. Early ladies' exhibitions played to invitation-only female audiences of as many as 500 people in the club gym. By 1910, however, both sexes and all ages were performing

on the same bill, and the doors were open to everyone with the price of admission. MAAC's public extravaganzas had become an opportunity to show how healthy and talented its members were.

The grand staging talents of Robert Krohn and his charismatic successor, O.C. Mauthe, were responsible for building the popularity of the exhibitions. With their knack for artistic effect, dramatic color schemes combined with stirring music and grand gestures to amaze the audience, usually 2,500 to 4,000 strong.

What the audience saw was some 400 to 600 Multnomah athletes entering in a grand processional of red and white, followed by group dances, drills with dumbbells, wands and sticks, fencing, as well as table vaulting, boxing and wrestling, "aesthetic movements," exhi-

Under Professor O.C. Mauthe, club members showed their physical talents in large-scale exhibitions. Mrs. D.H. Welch and Mrs. A.R. Bohosky performed as a Dutch girl and boy.

bition volleyball and gymnastics and other athletic endeavors.

Favorites among the gymnastics exhibitions were the Sawdust Brothers, a MAAC tumbling team proclaimed as good as any professional vaudeville team by the newspapers, and known for its artful pyramids. Children frequently provided the evening's ''cuteness quotient,'' portraying woodland sprites, forget-me-nots and fireflies.

While the spring exhibitions featured performances by Multnomah members only, the club often joined with groups such as Portland Hunt Club and Turn Verein to produce a Society Circus to benefit charity. The 1903 circus, held on Multnomah Field, offered athletic competitions (often featuring Multnomah athletes), messenger-boy speed contests, concerts, log rolling, and a carnival midway complete with ''freaks.'' Adding to crowd appeal were the mischievous antics of a Kangaroo Court, which held

lively mock trials of civic leaders. Board minutes relate that the 1910 circus, ''to be given jointly by the Multnomah Club and the Portland Hunt Club during the Rose Festival, will be the most pretentious affair of the kind ever attempted on the Coast. . . . Arrangements have been completed for the attendance of a band of Nez Perce Indians as one of the main attractions.''

The 1910 circus featured 500 performers and drew 15,000 people to three shows on Multnomah Field; 10,000 are said to have been turned away despite stormy weather. More than $8,000 was raised for charitable purposes. The 1927 Society Circus, held at the Ice Coliseum, was ''Better 'N Barnum,'' The Oregonian wrote. Its 45 acts included horseback riding, dancing and acrobatics.

Whether it was the effects of the Depression or the retirement of Mauthe in 1928, attendance at the exhibitions and circus began to dwindle. By 1931 the great era of exhibitions came to an end.

The Sawdust Brothers, circa 1894, were some of the club's earliest entertainers displaying acrobatic skills.

Phillip Neer

MAC

With coaching from "Terrible Ted" Thye, wrestlers led club sports in the 1920s. From local matches in the smoke-filled Heilig Theatre to the 1924 Olympic Games in Paris, MAAC matmen racked up local, regional and national championships, and brought home Olympic medals.

Robin Reed took up wrestling in high school to escape calisthenics, and at 18 won his first national title in the 125-pound division. With several Oregon Open, PNA and Pacific Coast championships from 1921 to 1924, he prevailed in the featherweight finals match of the 1924 Olympics against teammate *Chester "Chet" Newton* at 134½ pounds. The two were forced to face each other when one failed to make his usual weight class. The gold-silver finish of these friends earned a story in *Ripley's Believe It Or Not*.

Newton kept teammate *Robert Kruse* from a shot at the Olympic Games entirely, challenging the 192-pound wrestler in his weight class during a qualifying match. It was widely believed that Kruse, who had earned state and national championships, would have taken a medal had he reached Paris.

One former MAAC wrestler, *Russell Vis*, did take a gold. Vis, who trained eight years at MAAC until 1920 under Eddie O'Connell, won in the lightweight class. He wore Los Angeles Athletic Club colors, though, since he was attending college in the area.

Cyril Mitchell and *Ben Sherman* dominated MAAC wrestling after the 1924 Olym-

Ben Sherman

Tommy O'Brien

pics. Sherman took several state and PNA championships in various weights.
Mitchell, who competed at both 118 and 123 pounds, won the national AAU
title in 1926 and later coached at the club, molding national championship teams
in 1953 and 1965. He served four terms on the U.S. Olympic Committee

Robin Reed

for wrestling and was national
AAU Junior Olympic wrestling
chairman.

Leading the way in box-
ing was 18-year-old *Tommy
O'Brien*, who accumulated
an impressive 13-1 record and
three titles in 1923 — city,
Northwest, and Pacific Coast

Ralph Spearow

amateur champion. Described by his coach as the greatest fighter in the world
"for his inches and his ounces," his career was brief and limited to the
Northwest.

Better known nationally was tennis player *Phil Neer*, ranked at the age
of 18 as the Northwest's best. This earnest young man once nearly forfeited
a Portland match to fulfill his obligation to deliver newspapers. He went on
to take championships in Oregon, British Columbia, and
Ojai Valley, California, and was a finalist in international
competition.

In track and field, discus thrower *Gus Pope* took third place in the 1920
Antwerp Olympics and was later named to the All-American Team. He placed
first at the 1922 AAU meet.

Ralph Spearow, a pole vaulter, was expected to achieve Olympic glory
in the 1924 Games, having placed second nationally in 1922. He injured his
foot on the trip to Paris, however, and placed sixth at 12 feet 1¾ inches.
Spearow's greatest glory came on his return through Japan, where he set an
incredible — and unfortunately, unofficial — record of 15 feet ½ inch, clearing
it five times.

Chester Newton

1930-1939

FACING HARD TIMES

"If pleasures are greatest
in anticipation, just remember that
this is also true of trouble."

ELBERT HUBBARD

Trade Multnomah stadium for the old Lincoln High School property in the South Park Blocks? Before the October 1929 stock market crash, the notion would have seemed preposterous.

But, in the spring of 1930, the rapidly spreading rumor was the first public sign of MAAC's financial troubles. The August 6, 1930, *Oregonian* insightfully advised that such an exchange "would extricate both the schools and the club from difficulties that are bound to become more pressing...." There would be more talk of relocation before the Depression was over.

Multnomah faced formidable odds. The stadium had not had a major tenant since its construction, despite Aaron Frank's involvement. The club had lost more than 25 percent of its membership, some 400 departing in the three months following the October 1929 stock market crash. Existing and prospective members were angered and discouraged by the 10 percent federal tax on dues. Account delinquencies mounted. So did club debt.

The first Father-Son Dinner was implemented by A.B. McAlpin in 1931. About 400 attended and another 50 were turned away, according to newspaper coverage of the event. The turnout emphasizes the event was well received.

Members' contributions softened much of the 1930 operating loss of $12,000; borrowed money paid the $34,000 in accrued annual bond interest. For the first time in club history, the dining room, under the direction of Dorothy Styles, operated at a profit.

Still, stopgap measures and small victories could not halt the continuing slide. More concerted action was needed.

CHAPTER OPENING PHOTO: Membership drives were common throughout the 1930s. All kinds of promotions were employed in order to stabilize the membership base. Here, club members who served as recruiting team captains are seated with others at a 1930 dinner at the Multnomah Hotel.

The Oregonian's L.H. Gregory anticipated the situation prior to James J. Richardson's arrival in 1928: "The stadium is idle too much," he opined. A well-known sportsman, civic activist and promoter, "one of Richardson's duties as manager will be to increase business in every possible legitimate way," Gregory wrote.

The Pacific Coast Conference's promise of games in the stadium never fully materialized; the professional Portland Baseball Club ignored MAAC's 20-year lease proposal. To fill the void, Richardson found uses not contemplated by the arena's designers, some more successful than others. The temporary dirt track for motorcycle racing remained just that. While competitors could endure six-day bicycle races, audiences could not.

Exhibition boxing matches with Jack Dempsey, however, were an unqualified hit.

Ultimately, the answer to the stadium's viability came from the Oregon Legislature, which legalized pari-mutuel betting early in 1933. The Multnomah Kennel Club signed a five-year lease to pay $350 a day for an annual 60-day racing season; 30 days later, racing began.

MAAC MEMBERSHIP MADE EASY

Richardson's real talents were revealed in programs designed to sustain membership in the face of an annual turnover exceeding 20 percent. Fall membership drives were as predictable as November rain. The first was conducted by the J.H. Lang Agency of San Francisco. Later, the club hired Bob Peacock, at $75 a month, to call on businessmen directly.

Still later, enticements such as dues credits, new car raffles and life memberships drew a members-only volunteer recruitment corps.

Never had it been so easy to join MAAC. During most of the decade no initiation fee was charged if a new member paid the first three months' dues — typically $2.50 to $5.50 a month — in advance. Members joined and dropped out by the hundreds monthly; a revolving-door practice, if not policy, had been effected.

Recognizing the importance of membership stability, club leaders sought to end the constant

Club holdings appraised at $1.7 million secured $550,000 in gold bonds issued in 1925. Unretired debt from 1910 bonds, like the one at left, was refinanced by the 1925 sale.

JAMES J. RICHARDSON

He had many careers — salesman for Spalding sports gear, professional baseball scout, sports editor for The Oregonian. *But James J. Richardson, son of a San Francisco steamship magnate, found his true calling managing and promoting MAAC and its stadium.*

Founder of the Breakfast Club, a boosters' group, Richardson for years emceed their rousing Tuesday morning broadcasts over KGW radio. He furthered MAAC interests through this forum and his affiliations with the March of Dimes, the Rotary Club, the Rose Festival and others.

Richardson's loyalty to MAAC was stalwart. Weathering a pay cut prior to his honeymoon, he confided in a letter to President George Black, "I DO NOT want to leave...MORE money is NOT the consideration....Personally, I love the work."

During his tenure from 1928 to 1948, Richardson, an avid boxing fan, brought numerous boxing championships to the city. He served on AAU and Olympic boxing committees and many local boards. Said one member who knew him, "Jimmy was a very tough act to follow."

George Black, center, with Zina Wise and
C.B. Stephenson at a 1940 Old-Timers' Night.

GEORGE BLACK

*If you couldn't pay a $440,000
debt, spending $14,000 on renovations
might seem foolish. But George Black
Jr. believed the expenditure was vital to
the future of the club.*

*As active on MAAC committees
as he was on the tennis and handball
courts, Black was club president in
1935 in the midst of the club's default
on its massive stadium debt.*

*Allied with the board and Manager
James Richardson, Black convinced the
bondholders' committee that the club
facility was an asset to be maintained,
or members would cease to be attracted
to it. The renovations and a new
emphasis on family memberships
contributed to the club's turnaround.*

*A few years after his presidency,
Black helped Calvin Souther convince
members to buy back the defaulted
stadium bonds which were on the
market for 25 cents on the dollar. The
purchase nearly put to rest the adver-
sarial relationship between the club and
the bondholders' committee.*

turnover. First, trustees created the family membership in 1932. In 1933 Emil
Piluso was hired to reduce fluctuations by introducing new members more fully
to club activities. In 1934, he created the annual Totem Pole trophy competition with the Washington Athletic Club. Equal parts serious athletics and pure
fun, it remained popular until World War II interrupted.

As the nation went, so went Multnomah. When the Dow Jones average
plunged to a record low 42 in 1932, MAAC troubles piled higher. It needed
1,250 senior members to prosper, but had a stable base of only 550 or so. Business manager F.S. Miller reported a $1,600 payroll shortfall. The club account
with Graziano, Portland Heights' horse-cart produce vendor, regularly carried
a balance due of $1,600 to $1,800 a month.

In early 1932, for the first time in its history,
Multnomah defaulted on its funded debt. Despite
members' valiant efforts, the club could not carry
the substantial expense of the stadium.

The fallout was immediate. Bondholders
formed a committee, joining the stadium association and the club in grappling for Multnomah's

*"Sunbathing is healthy" was the common
belief when the club opened its solarium.*

meager income. Salaries were cut. All activities that were not financially self-
sufficient ceased. Of all competitive sports at MAAC, only boxing survived.
Money once spent on teams and representative athletes was instead used to
develop intramural activities. Even the bowling alleys and several pool tables
were ultimately removed and sold. The intent was to provide the most members
enjoyment at the least expense.

As the '30s advanced, Multnomah slowly came to grips with the fact
that its role had changed substantially. Once, the club provided the community
with a team and a place for competition. Colleges and professionals now filled
that niche. Recreational and social activities now dominated member interests.

By mid-decade, nagging doubt became general consensus: the clubhouse
itself had deteriorated badly. The only change in at least 10 years had been the
addition of an "indoor solarium." Noting the situation, outgoing president
George Black wrote, "The difficulty is not in procuring members, but in holding
them." Peeling paint, broken windows, tattered rugs, threadbare upholstery and
leaky plumbing did not induce allegiance. ▶ *page 80*

As entertainment, boxing packed a powerful punch. From the club's earliest years, fisticuffs were a regular feature of men-only evening ''smokers,'' on a bill of fare that included wrestling, acrobatics, music and short acts or skits. By the 1930s, though, smokers had become almost exclusively boxing events, with an occasional mixed card of boxing and wrestling.

During the Depression, Multnomah held six to 10 boxing smokers a year, and fighters represented the Winged M in matches sponsored by other local clubs as well. Admission was usually 50 cents, with an occasional ''Depression'' price of 40 cents, though the tab jumped to 75 cents when the club helped bring boxers from San Francisco. Members and the general public, women included, were welcome to crowd into the hot, haze-filled club gymnasium, inhale the aroma of sweat and cigar smoke and watch the action.

What was social entertainment for the crowd was athletic opportunity for the fighters.

No titles were up for grabs, and there were no cash rewards, but boxers valued the practice time and the chance to earn trophies. Many young fighters got their first taste of competition, including ''Hard Luck'' Tommy Moyer, who boxed in his first club smoker in 1934. Most important, boxers who made good in their fights were often invited to participate in state and regional AAU competitions.

Because club Manager James J. Richardson promoted Multnomah smokers so successfully, the club also hosted a number of official tournaments. The 1929 Pacific Coast Amateur Boxing Championships, held at the Portland Armory, were a huge success, drawing more than 8,000 fans, and the 1932 Far West Amateur Championships brought the club a small profit. But in 1934 MAAC took a loss of several hundred dollars hosting the Pacific Coast matches. It became clear MAAC's own smokers were more profitable to the club than the championship events. Smokers continued in popularity until World War II interrupted, carrying many fighters and much of the audience off to battle.

George Willey fought at 147 pounds.

THE STADIUM GOES TO THE DOGS! FROM 1933 THROUGH 1955, THE MULTNOMAH KENNEL CLUB LEASED THE STADIUM FOR ITS RACING SEASONS. DOG RACING BECAME POSSIBLE WITH THE LEGALIZATION OF PARI-MUTUEL BETTING. MURRAY KEMP, A FRIEND OF JIMMY RICHARDSON'S, SAW THE BILL THROUGH PASSAGE. IT WAS APPROVED AFTER KEMP ARRANGED TO HAVE A SHARE OF THE REVENUE DEVOTED TO SUPPORTING STATE AND COUNTY FAIRS AND SIMILAR EVENTS. THE FIRST THREE YEARS AFTER LEGALIZATION, THE GREYHOUNDS EARNED $225,000 FOR THE STATE. BUT, BY THE EARLY '50S, ANTI-GAMBLING SENTIMENT WAS BUILDING THROUGHOUT PORTLAND. THE DOGS THAT HAD SEEN THE CLUB THROUGH THE BLEAK YEARS STARTED TO GET SECOND BILLING TO OTHER EVENTS, SO THEY MOVED THEIR RACES OUT TO PORTLAND MEADOWS.

Astonishingly, a fund for capital improvements and repair had never been established. The stadium, however, remained the source of and solution to Multnomah's problems.

DESPERATE TIMES, DESPERATE MEASURES

On May 20, 1935, in a watershed meeting, the trustees, led by George Black, unanimously issued an ultimatum to the bondholders' committee: reduce the financial burden or the club would abandon the property. The owner of the new Elks Temple at Southwest 11th and Alder had offered "a fair and reasonable proposition for the housing of [MAAC] . . . and to assist this club in financing the same on an attractive basis. . . ."

The fans loved the dogs. When the popular Fawn Warrior ran, 33,000 attended. During World War II, benefits were held regularly for the George White Service Center.

The bondholders had earlier threatened foreclosure; the trustees now called their bluff. They knew that closing for any reason would cause the club and its property to lose tax-exempt status. Then, the taxes alone would deprive bondholders of both investment and collateral. The trustees also argued that the stadium association, well off due to the success of dog racing, was using all revenues from the stadium to pay bondholders. The stadium violated its contract by neglecting to pay rent to the club and participate in the club's upkeep. The club wanted to negotiate a compromise.

The trustees argued that the club's overall rehabilitation served everyone's best interests. They proposed bond interest payments be cut in half for '35 and '36, and that up to $34,000 of all excess net stadium income be devoted to renovations of the clubhouse. The board also recommended that from 1937 forward, the interest rate remain at 3 percent and any excess money be used to purchase outstanding bonds on the open market — often available at 20 to 25 cents on the dollar. Major bondholders would then recover at least the face value of their investments, a remarkable achievement in those times.

The bondholders capitulated. MAAC responded with an "atmosphere of enthusiasm" that President Black said in a letter to the bondholders' committee was "impossible to put in writing." Multnomah would survive.

The club ended the year showing a profit of $6,230. The closing of the long-troubled Multnomah Golf Club went almost unnoticed.

School children carry placards bearing the names of their grade schools during a '30s stadium pageant.

RULES 'MODERNIZED'; ALCOHOL ALLOWED

More changes were in store. In their first major revision since MAAC's founding, the bylaws were, as President Zina Wise put it, "modernized" in 1936. Despite some protests, alcohol was permitted for the first time — three years after repeal of Prohibition. Members could rent bottle lockers for $3 a year and pay set-up charges for cocktail service.

The bylaws were changed to permit stadium gambling, ending a situation of open violation of the original charter. A motion to allow slot machines in the club was vetoed; curiously, they would soon be installed at MAAC and many other Portland clubs.

▶ *page 83*

An erstwhile promoter, club Manager Jimmy Richardson, sixth from left, was the savior of the stadium. Dog racing was one of many uses Richardson found for the stadium. Here he is shown in front of the Portland Hotel with Aaron Frank and E.D. Smith Jr., third and fourth from left. These 1931 Challenge Day "arrests" hyped ticket sales for the Oregon vs. Washington football game.

TOM LOUTTIT

Thomas A. Louttit excelled in every sport he tried — football, baseball, basketball, boxing, wrestling, hockey and dog racing. Some men are natural athletes; Louttit, however, was also a natural referee. And coach and cartoonist.

A former MAAC Northwest boxing champion and football star, Louttit turned to coaching at age 24 in 1920. By 1923, his boxers had won 38 regional and national championships with a combined win-loss record of 149-43.

Louttit found his greatest success as a nationally ranked boxing referee and top Pacific Coast Conference football official. He "drew the call for...two Rose Bowl games, 136 major intersectional contests and a full annual schedule...for a 22-year period...."

Louttit was also recognized as a sports illustrator for The Portland News-Telegram *and* The Winged M.

With the 1933 arrival of dog racing in the stadium, Louttit was an obvious choice for race judge. He was named steward of the Oregon State Racing Commission several years before his death in 1951.

"How times change!" wrote The Oregonian's L.H. Gregory in 1924 regarding golf's popularity, and the appearance of golf pants in the staid old Multnomah Club lobby. *"Ten years ago a gent appearing in same would have been requested kindly to don his gym suit for decency's sake. How time do fly, how civilization do progress, how we improve — or do we?"*

Civilization aside, many MAAC members demanded the *"improvement"* of the club's own golf course. With just two in the city and one under construction as Gregory wrote his column, greens were crowded, and the Waverley and Portland clubs were members-only. Golf's popularity stole new MAAC prospects; craftier members wreaked havoc on dues income by resigning in the spring to devote themselves to golf, knowing they could return during fee-waived fall membership drives.

In 1924, MAAC's golf committee chose a $118,000 Raleigh Park site between Beaverton-Hillsdale Highway and Canyon Road, some five miles from MAAC by car, trolley or bus. A golf annex was established with its own directors, and by April, 500 club members had subscribed.

For $300 initiation and $5 a month in addition to regular dues, members got a tournament-quality course complete with water hazards and sand traps. But once it opened in 1925 it quickly became clear more members, and elimination of the MAAC membership requirement, were needed for the annex to thrive. In 1926, the Multnomah Golf Club separated completely.

Though the golf club showed promise, the Depression made its large new debt an overwhelming burden, and the club went into receivership in 1935. Had it still been part of MAAC, its financial woes, compounded with those of the stadium, could have brought down the entire club.

The view looking west from the Multnomah golf clubhouse porch was of the ninth green and the 10th tee and fairway, at center. Today, the former course is home to houses. The Raleigh Park Pool is just south of the site of the old clubhouse.

By 1936, the trustees believed the term "amateur" had lost its positive connotations. So, the club's moniker became the Multnomah Athletic Club — or, simply, MAC.

That year, membership reached an all-time high.

As the decade closed and the Depression ebbed, MAC regained strength. Clubhouse repairs and renovations proceeded. A slick monthly *Winged M* magazine replaced the weekly *Bulletin*. The initiation fee was reinstated, further stabilizing membership.

Even after repairs, the club was once again operating with an annual net income.

In 1938, the stadium lease with the kennel club was renewed at $550 per racing day. MAC also entered a new agreement with the bondholders' committee: maturity was extended to 1952 and interest lowered to 2 percent, which allowed funds for ongoing renovation and bond purchase.

Of all activities, competitive sports suffered most during the Depression. Hockey and soccer, popular at the start of the decade, died by its end. Wrestlers, boxers and weightlifters won national titles, but only boxers gained the glory of earlier days.

Two new sports did emerge. In 1930, Martin Arlberg and Thor Leaf represented the club in its first ski tournament. Skiing maintained a small but visible audience throughout the decade. By 1934, Portland skiers received shortwave radio reports from Mount Hood. Also, early in the decade, Al Tauscher returned from a California colloquium to teach members a new English game: badminton.

Skiers convert their transportation to the mountain into a convenient rope tow up it.

One constant remained, however, through those difficult years: Jack Cody continued to produce champions. Once he had given the Northwest the divers by which others were judged. Now came swimmers, led by a tiny young girl who began her career by winning a battle with polio. Soon, America would know Nancy Merki and her teammates simply as the Cody Kids.

M A C
C H A M P I O N S

Though boxing dominated the Depression, the club's only athlete at the 1932 Olympic Games was a weightlifter. *Arne Sundberg*, son of a railroad contractor, lifted steel rails, railroad ties and bridge spars before joining MAAC. He won a string of national weightlifting championships starting in 1926 — including some in heavier classes. As U.S. amateur light-heavyweight champ in 1930, he set three records. In 1932, he was the first athlete to compete in the entire Olympics, placing fifth as a lightweight.

Two years later, MAAC's *Gino Quilici* won the national amateur 181-pound weightlifting championship in New York in his first national meet. Quilici, the 1933 Pacific Northwest champion, was one of only nine U.S. men in his day to lift more than 300 pounds in the two-hand clean and jerk.

Barely missing the '32 Olympics was bantamweight boxer *Freddy Lynch*, 1930 Far Western champ. As 1932 Pacific Coast champ at 126 pounds, he made it to the Olympic team trials, but lost his second fight in the finals. A trip to nationals in 1934 had similar results.

That same year, boxer *Tommy Moyer*, 15, began a career that earned him the nickname "Hard Luck" Tommy. "Injury or unjust decisions five times denied him a national amateur title," said a 1941 *Winged M* article. "Even the boys who have won decisions over him, openly and graciously acknowledge that Tommy should have...."

"Relentless, determined, hurtful in attack," Moyer boxed in his first club smoker in 1934, and took his first title a year later at the Pacific Northwest Golden Gloves Tournament in Multnomah Civic Stadium. A four-time AAU finalist, Moyer brought home MAC's first national boxing title in 1941. As an

Arne Sundberg

amateur he amassed an astonishing 146-10-0 record. Moyer's most vivid memory was of his one fight stopped due to injury; the cut over his eye was slight compared to his wounded spirit. Remarkably, Moyer was never floored.

Hard luck apparently gone, Moyer went on to an outstanding professional career of 22 wins, no losses after joining the army in 1942.

In handball, *Rudie Weiss, Carl Dahl* and *John Cebula* stand out. As a doubles team, Weiss and Dahl won second place at the Pacific Northwest handball championships in 1931. Weiss left Multnomah after 1934 to compete for B'nai B'rith. Dahl was handball chairman at the club from 1932-34 and served as club president in 1949.

The Pacific Northwest doubles champion with *C.J. McAllister* in 1933, Cebula's main achievements were in singles. He took the Pacific Northwest singles title in 1929, 1930, 1931 and 1933. "His speed was phenomenal, his kills were frequent, and his excellent generalship in the court was evident," said *The Winged M* of Cebula's 1930 PNA conquest. While PNA victories qualified Cebula for nationals, he never placed; in 1931 he was unable to compete "due to an injury sustained when hitting a wall during PNA competition."

Virgil Cavagnaro carried forth MAC's wrestling dynasty. The state AAU wrestling champ seven times in 10 years beginning in 1937, he took titles at 175 and 191 pounds and heavyweight. A strong contender for the 1940 Olympic team, Cavagnaro led a four-man MAC squad to nationals in 1939 and was first at 191 pounds. MAC's *Hillis Schlappi*, at 123, placed third nationally. *Herb Hutton*, 145, and *Walter Arndt*, 174, were state champs that year.

Though the fame of the Cody Kids was still in the future, Jack Cody's protégés were already making a splash. *Hazel Olmstead* took second in the 1930 national women's junior fancy diving at Long Beach, the same year *Maxine Seelbinder* set a Pacific Coast record in the 200-yard breaststroke and began winning at city and state swim meets. Seelbinder placed second in backstroke in PNA competition although it was not her usual event. In 1934, she swam with *Virginia Shanafelt* and *Lois Murfin* to win the girls' medley 300-yard relay at the national junior championship.

Tommy Moyer

John Cebula

Virgil Cavagnaro

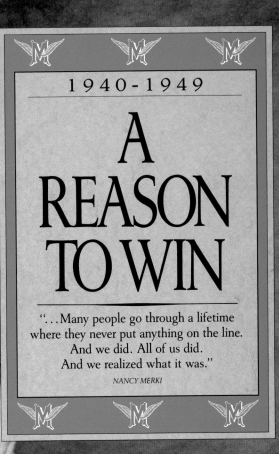

1940-1949

A REASON TO WIN

"...Many people go through a lifetime where they never put anything on the line. And we did. All of us did. And we realized what it was."

NANCY MERKI

MAC
TIMELINE

1940

PENICILLIN USED AS ANTIBIOTIC
PORTLAND AIRPORT MOVES FROM
SWAN ISLAND TO PRESENT SITE
SWIMSUITS REQUIRED FOR MALE
MAC MEMBERS

1941

U.S. SAVINGS BONDS AND STAMPS ON SALE

1942

FIRST COMPUTER MADE IN U.S.

1943

ITALY SURRENDERS TO ALLIES
U.S. RATIONS COFFEE, SUGAR, MEATS,
CHEESE, CANNED GOODS, SHOES

1944

D-DAY
U.S. COST OF LIVING RISES 30 PERCENT

1945

JAPANESE BOMB EXPLODES IN
KLAMATH COUNTY
GERMANY SURRENDERS
FIRST ATOMIC BOMB

1946

TWENTY-ONE NATIONS ATTEND
PEACE CONFERENCE

1947

INDIA PROCLAIMS INDEPENDENCE
FROM ENGLAND
FLYING SAUCER SIGHTINGS REPORTED
THROUGHOUT U.S.
BASEBALL PLAYER JACKIE ROBINSON
IS FIRST BLACK IN MAJOR LEAGUES
PORTLAND STERNWHEELER BUILT

1948

GANDHI ASSASSINATED
GOLDMARK INVENTS LONG-PLAYING RECORD

1949

MINIMUM WAGE IS 75 CENTS PER HOUR
PORTLAND CHILDREN'S MUSEUM OPENED

The worst times were over. Multnomah met the decade with a fresh look and improving finances. More than 1,500 invited guests came on a crisp October night in 1940 to be dazzled by MAC's new lower "luxury floor," just completed. The main floor remodeling was completed the year before as part of a major renovation. With the new steam room, innovative quiet room and other "ultramodern" amenities, MAC placed in the pantheon of American athletic clubs. The hard-won 1935 agreement with the bondholders was paying off.

More changes and improvements were to come. The long-anticipated Men's Grille opened in 1941, displacing the old card room. It served an average of 5,000 meals a month in its first year. The club's first electrical public address system eased the work of harried pages. And in 1945, a new, meticulously tiled swimming pool was completed. The

Founding president A.B. McAlpin cuts a massive cake marking the club's 50th anniversary. With him at the March 12, 1941, event is Jack Luihn, caterer of the old Sealy-Dresser Company.

work culminated with the 1948 opening of the new dining room. More than 2,000 guests attended the largest club party to date.

Operating on a cash basis with no past-due debts, MAC actually accelerated its construction projects after war was declared in December 1941. "This seemed wise," noted President Ronald C. Honeyman, "as a means of maintaining the present celerity of our activities and of thus offsetting loss of members...." The wisdom of such strategy would be borne out by war's end.

Dog racing's popularity guaranteed that stadium bonds would be retired without further difficulty. By 1949, the stadium association had increased the kennel club's rent to $100,000 per 60-day season, almost five times the original fee. Club slot machines also contributed a tidy profit – up to $73,600 per year. MAC ended the decade with its first million-dollar year.

The combined successes of stadium and club resulted in President Milo K. McIver's 1949 announcement of a new epoch: for the first time since 1891, Multnomah was debt-free.

CHAPTER OPENING PHOTO: Lifting America's spirits during World War II with their winning ways were the Cody Kids. While their ranks changed throughout the years, the most famous foursome was Nancy Merki, Brenda Helser, Suzanne Zimmerman and Joyce Macrae.

The growth of family memberships in the '40s continued to push the club away from a competitive athletic orientation. Social events ran the gamut from the risque to the respectable. Stag "mixers," complete with burlesque "girly-girly shows," did not outlive the decade despite their popularity with men. Club-sponsored dances open to non-member guests strained facilities but not goodwill. The All-Sports Dinner, the Father-Son Dinner, the Christmas Formal and the Mother-Daughter Tea were destined to become traditions.

In an echo of its past, a Men's Glee Club was tentatively approved in 1941 — this time without mandolins. The artistic success of this all-male chorus soon earned it official approval and a professional director.

With MAC approaching its 50th anniversary, 1941 was well-suited to nostalgic remembrances. The auspicious event was anticipated by the first Old Timers' Night Dinner, open to former presidents and trustees.

On Wednesday, March 21, 1941, 500 club members commemorated Multnomah's golden anniversary with a banquet in the gymnasium. Speakers included the governor, the mayor and the state penitentiary warden; the Cody Kids were guests of honor. First president A.B. McAlpin cut a massive, multi-tiered cake

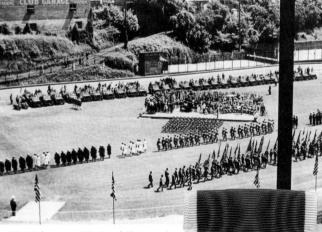

This July 1944 War Bond Show in the stadium included representatives from various branches of the armed services. The jeeps on the far side of the field held patients from Barnes Hospital. Note that tennis courts were still located on the east side of the field parallel to Southwest 18th Avenue. Use of the stadium was free whenever the cause benefited the war effort.

with the silver trowel used by Teddy Roosevelt at the 1911 cornerstone laying.

MAC had other reasons to celebrate that golden year. Its team of young women swimmers continued to galvanize national attention as they won tournaments and set national records across the country. Their athletic prowess, homegrown glamor, youth and vitality rocketed the Cody Kids into celebrity status.

VJ DAY

*The wait had been a long one —
nearly four years.*

*Multnomah members had anxiously
followed news of those serving in World
War II; "With the Colors," in* The
Winged M, *regularly reported on
"service suspense" members. Some 22
Multnomah men had given their lives.*

*Then at 4 p.m. on August 14,
1945, the longed-for news came. Club
radios were tuned in as President Harry
Truman announced Japan's uncondi-
tional surrender.*

*While throngs quickly crowded
downtown streets to rejoice, at Multnomah "the celebration was as intense,
but was more subdued," reported*
The Winged M. *In keeping with public
decree that bars close, the Men's Grille
shut down immediately, and remained
closed the next day.*

*Nonetheless, the 14th was "a joyous
night at the Club," with the dining
room filled to capacity. Sports activity
was limited, however. "It just wasn't
the kind of evening to play badminton,
or squash racquets," commented the
magazine.*

ANOTHER WAR TO FIGHT

"Since Pearl Harbor," *The Winged M* declared, "Red Cross Head-
quarters have been swamped with people wondering where they can best fit in.
Just as our boys are piling into recruiting stations, our women are offering their
services...." The club, no stranger to adversity, once more felt the strain of
war. So long concerned with internal needs, members now responded to the
needs of the country. MAC again started a flag bearing a star for each member
in the service.

With the impacts of World War I as learning experience, MAC was not
caught by surprise. Service-suspense membership, eliminating dues for club
members in active duty, had already been reinstituted in October 1940.
The following June the club proudly publicized "that out of the 30 odd
members...who have enlisted or who have been drafted, we haven't as yet
heard of a single rejection on account of physical examination." By Pearl Harbor,
December 7, 1941, the MAC Red Cross sewing unit was almost a year old.
A special fee-free membership category, Army and Navy, was created for
visiting GIs.

The new and popular glee club disbanded for the duration. "It was the
thing to do," said leader Dykeman White. "A majority of the members are doing
double duty...taking care of their own business and also putting in many hours
at the shipyards and other worthy war efforts." He called upon the newly formed
Women's Chorus, "those melody maids...[to] carry the old torch proudly."

At the government's request, almost all interclub activities and competition, save swimming, came to an immediate halt. MAC instead focused on
war readiness. Cyril Mitchell, Earl Biggs and others taught commando tactics
to members. Attendance levels in exercise classes shattered existing records.
"This is the admirable answer," Physical Education Director Al Tauscher stated,
"to whether or not the men and women of the country are cooperating with
the national physical defense program."

The war held a twist of fate for MAC's junior ski team. Schussing's
popularity had reached new heights; "natural color" movies of skiing at
Timberline attracted Saturday night crowds. But downhill proponents often
found the U.S. Army's mountain division at the base. No sooner had Bill
Healy been named ski team captain, reported *The Winged M*, than the Army

called. "Other members…are expected to follow as they reach their 18th birthdays." (The lure of skiing was strong for Healy; he later founded the resort at Mount Bachelor.)

The dedication of commodities and labor to the war effort denied members the use of their newly gained amenities. Shortages became common. Despite member pleas for just two mornings per week, fuel restrictions closed the new steam and hot rooms. Meat rationing put a quick end to special dinners and banquets. Meal service was discontinued in the Men's Grille. Gas rationing, dim-out regulations and a candy shortage canceled juniors' Christmas parties.

Despite obstacles, no one was willing to give up club dances in the gymnasium. "Restrictions on tires…gas…but not on fun at Your Club: Quit worrying about things. You can 'still travel'…and on a smooth floor at The Club!" Before war's end, lush new draperies were hung in the gymnasium to create a "swanky new nightclub" rivaling those seen in Hollywood movies. Curtained areas under the running track created 14 private alcoves. A special bar and larger dance floor completed the party atmosphere. The Fuchsia Room was born.

Each month, *The Winged M* repeated its role as conduit between civilian and service-bound members. The January 1942 cover proclaimed MAC's second call to arms with drawings of soldiers from both world wars. The July issue abandoned the normal magazine format, instead resembling an oversize envelope. It bore the address, "A Letter from Home to MAC Members in the Service," and an inscription: "We'd give anything to see you boys come bouncing up the Salmon Street steps!" The June 1943 cover asked blood donors, "Have you bled for those bleeding for you?" Its black-and-white photo of field hospital casualties "bled" red ink.

Winged M advertisements asked members to buy Victory Bonds and cigarettes — servicemen constantly needed smokes. The Red Cross implored members to supply or sponsor sundries-filled ditty bags for overseas soldiers. ▶ *page 94*

The war years were social ones for Multnomah. In a time when people felt deep need to pull together, what better place to find a sympathetic, supportive atmosphere than "Your Club"? Rationing and public policy may have cancelled everything from buffet dinners to interclub athletics, but people could still dance, sing or play.

At MAC, they did all three. Informal Friday night dances in the Mirror Room were promised as long as members showed support; they lasted through the decade. Holiday formals were also popular Mirror Room events, until the opening of the Fuchsia Room in October 1944.

"Fourteen alcoves surround the dance floor..." related The Winged M, detailing "the rich formality" of columns in fuchsia and eggshell, drapings of flame-proofed fuchsia, hurricane lamps on each table, and an orchestra grotto. Party-goers could easily forget they were in a disguised gymnasium. Members flocked to dance on the larger floor.

Starting the decade with a song was the Men's Glee Club. Though the war effort put a temporary crimp in membership, the Women's Chorus organized in 1943, and the sexes

The city's first Ugly Hat Contest was held at MAC in 1949. The winning entry consisted of Chinese lanterns and a parrot. Scouring pads and kitchen utensils make up the hat to the right.

sometimes joined forces. The men regrouped at war's end, soon changing their name to the Balladeers.

Starting with a 45-member minimum,

The Men's Glee Club enjoyed popularity in the early '40s but a declining number of singers during the war forced its members to disband. After the war, voices were in tune again and the men renamed themselves the Balladeers. They performed on stage with notables such as Bob Hope and Bing Crosby. But MAC banned singing in the bar.

membership in the Balladeers soon capped at 100 singers. So popular were these vocalists that they performed throughout the Northwest, for grand openings, Rose Festival, on radio, even for a March of Dimes Telethon with Jayne Mansfield. They perform to this day.

With the annual MAC-Washington Athletic Club interclub meet canceled in 1942, MAC staged its first Play Day, "to demonstrate to all members that vacations this summer will never be missed if they just take advantage of the sport facilities of The Club."

The members-only senior event was filled with activities from 10 a.m. until 2 a.m. the next day. Members were split into two teams, Reds and Blues, for skits, stunts, 18 athletic events, and women's bridge, all capped by a buffet dinner and informal dance. Points were kept, the Reds won — and a tradition was born.

"While we have many group tournaments throughout the year in which comparatively few members participate, 'Play Day' can become our big all-member gathering of the year," said President Dudley Clark. That it did, continuing well into the '50s. Many members said they enjoyed Play Day more than any interclub meet ever held.

Old-Timers' Night in November 1940 attracted former president Ferry Smith, charter member William F. Lipman, track great Edward E. Morgan and Frank G. Smith.

Interclub competitions added a social side to athletic competitions. Here, MAC members ready for the trip to the Washington Athletic Club in Seattle in April 1941. MAC lost the contest 25 to 75.

ONE-ARMED BANDITS

Two years after trustees first unanimously refused them, "one-armed bandits" found a lively clientele at MAC. In fact, nearly all major Portland private clubs had slot machines. If any stigma was attached, law enforcement officials who were MAC members never complained.

Slot owners made it easy, providing free machines for 25 percent of the take. MAC bettered that deal when it bought 14 of its own 25-cent machines from the Bell-O-Matic Company in Chicago in 1945-46. Conveniently placed in the club bar and locker rooms, the machines earned up to $73,600 annually despite the small stakes.

A city-wide sweep in the early '50s ended Portland clubs' shadow life.

Letters from members on both fronts told of hardship, heartache and hope. Navy Captain A.W. Wagner advised, "I can now walk down the deck 'on the bias' in a straight line without missing a step (or looking like an exit from a MAC party)." Dr. Sanford Wollin, who would serve as president in 1971, wrote of the sad state of the recaptured Philippines: "I've lost practically all of my underwear to the half-naked kids. The American GI...[would] give them all his food, clothing, etc., if the Army didn't put a stop to it." To a man, they all longed for the fellowship of the clubhouse.

The stadium was involved with the war effort from the outset. *The Winged M* reported "mammoth meetings of civil defense and labor groups to recruit their ranks." War Industries League football thrilled fans with professional-rules open-style games. A 1943 mock battle with infantry, bazookas, machine guns and mortars drew 3,500.

The club and the stadium collaborated in support of the George White Victory Center, which offered social services for soldiers in transit and war bond sales for patriotic investors. Recalling its turn-of-the-century vaudeville antics, MAC staged a benefit show on the center's rooftop. A kennel club racing series raised more than $100,000 in a six-day span. Bond drive shows were a regular occurrence at the stadium; no stadium rent was charged for any wartime fundraiser.

By 1943, the loss of more than 650 members' dues threatened club finances. Reluctantly, trustees raised dues. President Dudley Clark implored members to recruit replacements with offers of free two-week guest cards. The concern was premature. Due to the massive renovations and the 1940 creation of the associate woman category, by 1945 membership stood at an all-time high of 5,000. For the first time, all classifications were closed.

Demobilization led to the restoration of long-missed club luxuries. Less than five minutes after the announcement that fuel oil restrictions had been lifted, the steam room was reopened for use. As soldiers drifted home, protocol was established for transfer from service-suspense to active membership. The day after the Japanese surrender, thousands gathered in the stadium for prayer and thanksgiving. Multnomah's service flag bore more than 775 stars, 22 of them gold for those who made the supreme sacrifice. World War II had ended.

A NATION SHIFTS GEARS

With peacetime came an era of restoration and transition. Members returned to the clubhouse so desperately salvaged from the Depression. MAC filled its social and recreational mandate as a gathering place for parties and picnics. The Men's Glee Club, soon to be known as the Balladeers, re-formed with 50-plus voices. Popularity notwithstanding, the 1947 house committee barred them (and all others) from spontaneous singing in the Men's Grille.

Change, however, was pervasive. McAlpin died in 1946; few other charter members survived. Many longtime employees would soon leave.

Ben Templeton, club barber and raconteur for 30 years, was presented with a $25 Indian blanket and club membership upon his 1945 retirement. The most shocking departures, however, were Jimmy Richardson and Jack Cody. After 20 years of double duty, Richardson resigned as club manager in June 1948 to focus his attentions on the stadium. MAC immediately launched a nationwide search for his replacement.

One year later, Jack Cody announced his resignation after 36 years of producing world champions. His assistant of 34 years, Grace Kadderly DeBoest, preceded him in April.

Shoulder to shoulder, in 1949, MAC's athletic staff showed its strength. Pictured are Joe Loprinzi, who started in 1938; LeRoy Durst, who worked from 1948-90; Phill Hansel, 1949-56; Al Tauscher, 1923-83; Owen Carr, 1919-60; Jack Pobochenko, 1945-65; and Cyril Mitchell, 1929-83.

New faces soon became familiar. After a false start, a new manager was found in 1949; Verne Perry was destined to leave his substantial mark. Jack Cody's assistant and former MAC competitor, Jack Pobochenko, dove in as aquatics director, bringing Phillip Hansel with him as coach.   ▶ *page 98*

*S*oon after it turned 11, Multnomah helped set the stage for the birth of another organization destined to become a city institution: the Portland Rose Festival.

"The Portland Rose Club was granted the use of the field for the purpose of holding a rose carnival on two afternoons in June," read MAAC's board minutes of June 5, 1902.

The first floral parade, in 1904, was also staged from Multnomah Field. Its success led to a 1907 parade and official organization of the Rose Festival Association that year. Like Multnomah, Rose Festival was on its way to becoming a permanent fixture of city life.

From the start, the two groups had much in common, including members. In 1907, Tom Richardson, a festival committee member, invited Robert Krohn, MAAC's athletic instructor, to drill Portland school children for the parade. Champion MAAC tennis player Brandt Wickersham chaired the parade committee, serving with U.S. Bank owner J.C. Ainsworth, another MAAC man. Jimmy Richardson, retired two years from club management, was the 1950 association president. Since 1912, 44 club members have served as association president; O.W. Mielke presided for three terms. MAC sometimes sponsored a float, too, including one carrying the Cody Kids in 1940.

Multnomah Field helped cement the bond. It was so vital that the 1926 parade was canceled due to stadium renovations — one of just three cancellations in history. Queens of Rosaria received their crowns there. Rodeos, aquacades, ski jumping demonstrations and other events enthralled festival crowds. Most spectacular were the Rosaria pageants; one 1927 extravaganza featured 3,000 Persians, Greeks, knights, pilgrims and pioneers who changed costumes in tents, while club boilers blew a curtain of steam for the massive stage.

Rose Festival use of the stadium was considered a civic contribution; consequently, charges were low. In 1904, the cleaning fee was "not to exceed $5." In lean years, though the stadium was financially troubled, the Rose Festival used it free.

But in 1947, ties began to loosen. For the first time, the parade did not originate at the stadium. Officials believed larger floats would be used if they didn't have to negotiate the ramp. Unhappy stadium and club management cited "the convenience to the thousands of mothers, children, and old folks in particular, who could, by the purchase of a Rose Festival button, see the spectacle in comfort." In 1948, the Vanport flood forced the parade to the east side. And though the parade returned to the stadium throughout the '50s, possibilities for a stadium-parade connection ended forever with the 1960 opening of Memorial Coliseum.

Still, Multnomah had provided fertile ground for Portland's most enduring celebration, ensuring that "For you a rose in Portland grows."

Above: As early as 1912, MAAC had an entry in the Rose Festival Parade. Oliver K. Jeffery is the driver of this car. To his left is Lucille Bronaugh. Below: During the 1940s, purchasing a special Rose Festival button allowed entry to the stadium to view the start of the Grand Floral Parade. The club's involvement began in 1902 with the festival's fore-runner, the Rose Carnival. Numerous club members have served as officials of the Rose Festival Association and the Royal Rosarians.

MAC
MEMORABILIA

One smile quickly became a MAC institution. LeRoy Durst took over as club boxing coach and instructor on his 29th birthday in 1948, filling the vacancy left by champion-turned-coach Tommy O'Brien (himself a 1943 replacement for Tom Louttit).

With few notable exceptions, club sports continued to suffer through the '40s. The war all but ended serious interclub competition for men; those who would be athletes were most likely to be soldiers. The bright spots in an otherwise dreary decade were Tommy Moyer, national amateur boxing champion, and the celebrated Cody Kids. While MAC's astonishing successes in competitive weightlifting all but eluded public recognition, there was consolation when Owen Carr and Al Tauscher were acknowledged (some 20 years late) for being the first Americans to set world records in that sport.

Recreational sports thrived, especially indoors. *The Winged M* featured "bad" news: badminton had gained a prominent perch. Fencing returned after a 30-year hiatus. The more assertive table tennis supplanted lowly ping pong. The new, popular squash racquets replaced antiquated squash tennis, forcing court remodeling.

Badminton became the social sport of the 1940s. A Canadian demonstration team appeared at MAC in 1937, spawning interest. By 1949, Mary Anne Hansen Wolfe had won her first state singles and doubles titles. During the '50s, she took a singles or doubles title eight years.

Renascent tennis was almost lost in the fray. Sam Lee's third intramural tournament victory in 1940 gave him permanent possession of the 33-year-old Katz Cup; he donated a replacement trophy in 1942.

Despite competitive sport's continuing low estate, MAC's commitment continued. In 1945 the first junior membership merit awards were granted. Twenty grade school and high school students would receive scholarships to train at MAC in their best sport. Members served on numerous regional and national AAU and Olympic committees before, during and after the war.

MAC, once a men's club, faced new challenges as the family membership, nurtured since the 1910s, now had greater weight in establishing club policies. Suddenly, children were everywhere — in marksmanship classes, on the wrestling mat, in boxing lessons, camped out in the stadium. Trustees heard complaints of their rowdiness and occasional "thievery." Could or should the club accommodate them?

As 1950 approached, MAC facilities were still a concern despite a decade of extensive remodeling. Club property was no longer tax-exempt. An unstable market deflated early informal inquiries about real estate acquisitions and disposal of the burdensome stadium. To anticipate future needs and directions, the building and finance committee was founded in 1948.

Stressed by its resurgent success, MAC ended the 1940s with nearly 7,000 members and its first genuine post-war problems: parking and kids.

Great numbers of women attended new exercise programs initiated for them. The ladies drill in this gym class circa 1946.

JACK CODY

"Get the lead out of your pants."
Though Jack Cody was known to
unleash colorful epithets from poolside,
his coaching talent is recorded solidly in
black and white on the record books of
swimming and diving competition.

A world champion diver, Cody
produced some of the greatest aquatic
athletes of the 20th century during a
36-year career. Known for his sense of
humor, Cody is remembered as being
"boyish all his life."

Born in New York City, Cody
arrived in Portland in 1911 to coach at
the Natatorium at Southwest 12th and
Morrison. Two years later, aged 28, he
came to MAAC, making his first great
mark with divers. Several of his protégés achieved world renown in the
1920 Olympics. Louis E. "Hap"
Kuehn won a gold, and Thelma Payne
and Louis Balbach took bronzes.
Another '20s Olympic champion,
Norman Ross, had been a Cody
swimming pupil.

In the mid-1930s, the spark of
talent that grows to
Olympic proportions
ignited again.
Cody had been
coaching Nancy Merki
since she was 8, but
she couldn't compete
nationally until she
turned 12 in
1938. In 1939,
she stunned the
swimming world
as high-point
winner in the
nationals; she

(continued)

*Making headlines and filling full newspaper pages with their smiles were Cody Kids Joyce
Macrae, Nancy Lewis, Audra Haffenden, Anne Cooney, Nancy Merki, Brenda Helser and
Bernice Lindsay. This photo was splashed across a page of* The Oregonian *in 1939.*

Could today's athletes reach the top in a sport on less than three hours
of practice a week?

In the late '30s and the '40s, it was more than possible. It was the
schedule that catapulted Jack Cody's team of barely teen-age girls to acclaim
as the darlings of American swimming. During a 10-year period, the Cody Kids
racked up three national team crowns, a total of 58 national championship
events, plus American records and other honors in quantity — many of which
held for years.

With decades as MAC's swim coach, Cody knew his sport, and in the
mid-1930s he saw the makings of not just one outstanding swimmer but an
entire team.

Among them was *Nancy Merki*. A polio victim at age 7, she started
lessons to combat its effects, and was invited to MAC as an athletic member

at age 8. It was four years before AAU rules allowed her to compete nationally. Yet, in her first season, she was MAC's high scorer at the 1938 Far Western championships in San Francisco. *The Examiner* hailed her as "the most colorful swimmer on the program."

The next year, Merki set the sports world abuzz as high point scorer in the AAU nationals. By 1940 she was ranked No. 2 in the world in the 400-meter freestyle.

But Merki was not alone. MAC's second-place relay team at the '39 nationals included *Brenda Helser, Joyce Macrae* and *Anne Cooney*. The 1940 world rankings listed Helser third in the 400-meter and sixth in the 100-meter freestyle. Cooney was seventh in the 100-meter backstroke. Other outstanding Cody Kids included *Audra Haffenden, Bernice Lindsay, Nancy Lewis* and *Mary Anne Hansen*, record holders in their own right, and often on winning relay teams.

Later, a promising swimmer from Lake Grove would finally convince her mother to let her try for the team. *Suzanne Zimmerman's* lifetime of swimming in the lake brought her to the top in backstroke.

CODY'S KIDS
They are best swim team in U. S.

Cody's Kids are the four pretty high-school girls pictured above who hold all but one of America's freestyle relay swimming titles. Their real names are Nancy Merki, Brenda Helser, Suzanne Zimmerman and Joyce Macrae. But in Portland, Ore. where they live, these girls are known simply as Cody's Kids, so called for their famous coach, Jack Cody. The wiry 57-year-old instructor at the Multnomah Athletic Club believes that only scientific training and hard work can develop great swimmers. Behind the records of his Kids are long, monotonous hours of conditioning. They start with gym workouts, developing their muscles by weight-lifting. Once in the pool, they swim the length of the tank (25 yd.), gradually increasing the distance until they can swim it 72 times...

NANCY MERKI, BRENDA HELSER, SUZANNE ZIMMERMAN AND JOYCE MACRAE RELAX ON DOCK AT LAKE OSWEGO, NEAR PORTLAND, AFTER PRACTICING LONG-DISTANCE SWIMMING

CODY cont'd.

and Brenda Helser, Joyce Macrae and Anne Cooney scored second in relay. Asked at an early competition who the young swimmers were, a sportswriter said, "Those are Cody's kids." The name stuck.

What set Cody apart as a coach? "He was a master at the art of timing," said Merki later. "He knew what pace a swimmer should go out in the first 100 yards, the 200....Back in those days that kind of thing just wasn't done."

He was also a master of tactical psychology. One Kid who often worried her way out of winning fell asleep during a meet, and Cody left her alone. His last-minute bark to wake up got her adrenalin flowing; she jumped in the water and won.

Perhaps the greatest disappointment of Cody's coaching career was not being selected to coach the 1948 women's Olympic swim team, though three of his current or former swimmers were going. Since no Games had been held in '40 or '44, competition for the coaching spot was keen.

In 1949 Cody retired and moved to Los Angeles. When the invitation finally came to coach the 1956 women's Olympic swim team, poor health forced him to decline. Cody, who died in 1963, was inducted into the Oregon Sports Hall of Fame in 1990, joining several of his famous Cody Kids.

Life *magazine did a three-page spread on Jack Cody and his Kids in July 1942. Shown dockside are Nancy Merki, Brenda Helser, Suzanne Zimmerman and Joyce Macrae. The magazine article, complete with photos demonstrating stroke techniques, called the Kids "the best swim team in the U.S."*

MAC
MEMORABILIA

THE CODY KIDS COLLECTED WINNERS'
MEDALS THE WAY A GENERAL WORE
BRASS. THESE, SOME OF MARY ANNE
HANSEN'S NUMEROUS RIBBONS AND PINS,
ARE FROM THE 1938 AAU CHAMPIONSHIP
AND THE 1946 FAR WESTERN AAU
CHAMPIONSHIP. HANSEN'S FIRST
COMPETITION WAS AS A 13-YEAR-OLD IN
1938: SHE WAS A MEMBER OF THE RELAY
TEAM. A YEAR LATER, SHE GAINED
NATIONAL NEWS COVERAGE BY SUFFERING
BUTTON FAILURE ON HER SWIMSUIT TWICE.
SHE STILL PLACED FIFTH IN AN INDIVIDUAL
RACE AT THE NATIONAL OUTDOOR MEET
IN DES MOINES, IOWA. HER COMPETITIVE
SWIMMING CAREER CONCLUDED AT
THE NATIONAL INDOOR MEET IN
SEATTLE IN 1947.

The girls did not merely win meets; they broke record after record at dizzying speeds and sometimes sliced incredible amounts off earlier times. Zimmerman at one point held every backstroke record in the AAU book. Merki whacked an amazing 27 seconds off a previous world mark in the 1500 meter. As a team, the Cody Kids took nine national medley relay titles and set an American record, plus six national freestyle relay crowns and a world mark.

Practice time was restricted. Multnomah was still so much a man's club that many men swam nude. So Tuesday and Friday evenings, the girls entered Multnomah's ivy-covered walls, and waited in the library until 7 p.m. when they could go down to the pool.

There they did their "twenties" — three vigorous sets of 20 lengths, in the style Cody told them to swim, with short rests between. Next, Cody divided the girls into teams for competitive relays. Practice was over in an hour. The girls returned on Saturday mornings for more of the same. Before a meet they might swim an extra night or, in summer, go to the Jantzen Beach pool.

Though the Cody Kids were famous before World War II broke out, the war fostered their celebrity status. Photogenic and successful, they were a dose of happy news in a world dominated by battle. Photos in *Life* magazine and a cartoon on the cover of the *New Yorker* featured the all-American sweethearts;

Mary Anne Hansen and Bernice Lindsay handle the oars at Lake Oswego. Other Cody Kids are, in the bow, Nancy Lewis and Anne Cooney with Joyce Macrae and Brenda Helser in the stern.

Zimmerman's 1948 cover photo and story in *Collier's* earned front-page mention in *The Oregonian*.

Being a Cody Kid was an often heady experience. There was cross-country travel by train, and later plane, to AAU nationals. Defending champions got a free ride from the AAU. Expenses for other swimmers were covered by the club's Olympic fund. Club Manager Jimmy Richardson and well-known merchant Aaron Frank saw to it that the girls had the support they needed to concentrate on swimming.

Large crowds, led by Portland's mayor, turned out at Union Station. The girls were regular guests at ribbon cuttings, dinners and civic events. Merki, because of her early bout with polio, traveled to the White House in January 1942 for a March of Dimes event where Franklin Roosevelt, another polio victim and swimmer, personally took her to tour the White House pool.

If the war boosted their celebrity, it denied the Cody Kids the opportunity to swim in the 1940 and 1944 Olympics. The 1948 Olympics in London loomed as the last chance. Zimmerman, Merki and Helser, now in their 20s, made the team, though by this time Helser swam for a Los Angeles club.

Zimmerman won the silver medal in the 100-meter backstroke, trailing a Danish competitor by six inches, which was a slim margin in that meet. Helser was on the gold-medal relay team. For Merki, the Olympics came too late in her career. Recently married and recovering from a virus, she barely made the team, then placed seventh in the 400-meter freestyle.

Merki swam once more for soon-to-retire Cody in the 1949 indoor nationals, largely to help him raise funds for the next coach. She ended her career with the individual championship, and helped the team win two relays.

The Cody Kids, as usual, ended up as winners.

Too risque for use in Portland papers, this publicity photo was labeled for out-of-town use only. Protecting the modesty of the girls was important; Mrs. Cody always served as a chaperone on trips. From left are Suzanne Zimmerman, Marilyn Luper, Nancy Merki, Sharon Langdon, Billie Atherton, Joan Niesen and Margaret Deremer.

1950-1959

FAMILY
EVER
MORE

"Today we stand sound financially,
alive athletically, interesting socially —
an aggressive club in an expanding and
fast-moving section of this great country."

HENRY BALDRIDGE, MAC PRESIDENT 1952

MAC
TIMELINE

Perseverance had paid off. Multnomah entered the '50s debt-free and dressed up, setting local standards for post-war prestige. Financial ghosts exorcised, club leaders looked toward the future. For the first time, MAC was genuinely affluent. By 1954, the club netted $117,000 from its annual $2.2 million budget.

Multnomah's 50th anniversary in 1941 had been acknowledged modestly as a mark of endurance; the club had weathered turbulent times. Befitting the new prosperity, the club's 60th anniversary Starlight Party was billed as "the most gigantic undertaking ever attempted by MAC."

Bob Fulton's Security Sign Company contributed this sign for the anniversary celebration. KGW presented "Flight of the Winged M," and KEX recorded and rebroadcast the entire program in a special Sunday night feature.

Scheduled in June for warmer weather, the prime rib dinner and dance filled the stadium floor with 363 tables and 2,500 people. The neon Winged M sign, moved temporarily from the club entrance, decorated the field, along with a large sign near the north end zone proclaiming "60 Years." Strings of multicolored lights twinkled under a full moon. A KEX radio recording of the extravaganza made it all the more unforgettable.

STADIUM CONTINUES TO PERPLEX

At long last, MAC owned the stadium free and clear, with the final bonds retired in 1952. Yet, despite being debt free and despite a

The corner of Southwest 19th and Salmon is cleared for MAC's new parking lot, to come complete with lights, shrubbery, and yellow parking lanes.

long-term tenant, big promotions and grandstand improvements, the stadium continued to be a financial drain. Some even talked of selling.

The dream of top-rank football in the stadium never died, and the '50s finally brought successful booking of NFL exhibitions. The civil-war rivalry of Oregon and Oregon State returned after a 12-year hiatus, and other collegiate matches that had once eluded stadium and club leaders were scheduled.

CHAPTER OPENING PHOTO: The beginning and advanced dance classes come together for this December 1951 photo. Mr. and Mrs. Ed Cheney, center, taught all 200 men and women to dance every Monday night in the main lounge. The "Easy Ed Cheney Way" ballroom classes continued into the 1990s, taught by Dick and Dorothy Walker.

Operation Football boosted ticket sales with Kick-Off and Goal Post parties as well as post-game late-night dances.

But other stadium uses caused concern. For 20 years, Murray Kemp had run Multnomah Kennel Club's dog races free of any hint of scandal. The dogs accounted for more than 60 percent of total annual stadium attendance. But some members objected to any taint of gambling. MAC's slot machines had been removed; many believed dog racing should go too.

In 1953, at the end of a three-year lease, Multnomah bought the Gold-hammer property, the last remaining parcel within the 11-acre stadium-clubhouse tract not owned by the club. The stadium could now be expanded for professional baseball; the dogs had had their day.

The Portland Beavers played their first game at Multnomah Civic Stadium in spring 1955, bringing with them the infield turf from their old Vaughn Street home. "Unquestionably it will be a great moral lift," said President H.A. Weiss, "in being associated with the national pastime...."

Soon after the kennel club departed, stadium Manager James J. Richardson announced his retirement, ending a 27-year career affiliation with MAC. Verne Perry, like Richardson, would have a dual role managing both club and stadium.

BURGEONING MEMBERSHIP FORCES LOOK AT SPACE

Remain or relocate? Remodel or rebuild? "This...is a subject that has been studied by the Club trustees for many years," President George Halling told members in February 1954. Speculation now yielded to action, thanks to two recently formed committees. During the 1950 administration of Tom Stoddard, the building reserve fund was established; its work was buttressed the next year when the investment committee was formed by Henry E. Baldridge, president. His group's goals were explicit: to save $2.5 million to build a new clubhouse by 1972.

Above: Oregon State College beat the University of Washington 28-20 while a record-setting 32,890 people watched on November 3, 1956. Inset: Murray Kemp, president of the Multnomah Kennel Club, locks his office at Multnomah Civic Stadium as dog racing moves to a new location.

GUY THOMPSON

*When 700 men gathered for the
St. Patrick's Day stag party in 1950,
they celebrated a milestone: Guy
Thompson had become MAC's first
50-year employee.*

*Thompson, pictured here circa 1904,
came to MAC in 1900 and rose quickly
from bellboy to pin boy at Chapman
Street, earning $25 a month for a six-
day week. In those days, Thompson
"made the rounds" delivering state-
ments to save on postage. He put up the
first dollar to buy a club radio in 1922,
and was still around to greet television
30 years later.*

*Known as a "walking encyclopedia"
of sports statistics, Thompson was an
athlete in his own right. He placed third
in the 1905 Lewis & Clark Exposition
handball tournament (with T. Morris
Dunne first and Frank Watkins second).
Thompson gave handball lessons at
the club, where he later became night
manager.*

Halling, in 1954, proposed that expansion start as early as possible.
To do so required the sale of some or all of club property. In fact, confidential
solicitations had begun.

The need for larger quarters was obvious. In the early '50s, membership
stayed constant at 7,000-plus, with a steady climb in junior members. That
growth led first to the 1953 closure of junior membership, followed by establishing a senior family waiting list in 1956. Additional strain on facilities came
from divergent needs: juniors dominated athletic activities; seniors crowded
social ones.

In late 1953, Perry returned from an extensive tour of eastern clubs
with good and bad news. Yes, the club offered its members more activities,
both social and athletic, than almost any other club in the nation. But no,
Multnomah could not hold its vaunted status without adding a ballroom, a
new swimming pool, more handball and badminton courts – in short, "many
things which we in no way could house in the building we now occupy."

Architectural renderings for a proposed 65,000-square-foot east wing
were revealed in September 1956. The trustees' construction budget was based
on increased senior membership; new members would help fund the space to
accommodate them. Property acquisitions would end, and, wisely, stadium
income was not part of the budget.

In response, the 1957 board made membership expansion an immediate objective. Their goals were perhaps too easily met – membership grew
dramatically. By October, the total reached an all-time high of 8,700, one
third juniors. All categories were immediately frozen. Surely the new wing
was imminent.

But construction plans
were quickly dealt a double
blow. Inflation wreaked havoc
with budgeted costs; worse
yet, the federally proposed
"18th Avenue Freeway" route

▶ *page 112*

*This Meier & Frank model displays
the "sheer wools and colorful wraps"
that were described as "perfect for
parties before the stadium football
games." The 1954 fashion show was
part of the "Calendar of Fashions," a
colorful array of costumes selected to
tie in with year-round events at MAC.*

Above: MAC sponsored the first official ski race to open the 1950 season at Mount Hood on December 11. MAC's ski team made a good showing: back row, Larry Black, Oran Robertson, Bob Wochos; middle row, Dick Lewis, Dotti Maxwell, Pete Withers, Dick Ervin, Jack Warren; front, Kenny Van Dyke, Fredi Loll, Rees Stevenson, John Bosch, Bill Healy. Inset: The first MAC ski school started in February 1952, and busloads of members took to the slopes at Mount Hood.

A polar bear would think it a curious sight: grown men bobbing in a pool filled with 100-pound blocks of ice. Yet New Year's Day 1950 saw just such a scene as one of MAC's zanier traditions was born: the Polar Bears.

Originally intended as a "greeters' group," purpose did not become practice. The Bears simply preferred "goofing around," said King Blubber "Ham" Gerber, twice ruler of the Bears.

Chief outlet for the men's enthusiasm was water sports, and the March 1950 Winged M proclaimed, "The [Polar] Bears have started a new game known as water volleyball." They also continued the New Year's Day swim, with the ice blocks, plus a cargo net for bear-style climbing. Another

activity was seeing who could swim farthest with a lighted candle.

The Polar Bears carried out numerous exploits at Portland's zoo, where they tried for years to use the polar bear exhibit for an ice-cold swim. Thwarted by an alert and uncooperative Zero, then the resident polar bear, they usually had to settle for some other pool. But one year, when Zero's successors were cubs, they succeeded. Victory!

In 1955 the Polar Bears moved their New Year's swims to backyard pools or a jump from a boat in the middle of the chilly Willamette or Columbia. In 1974 they broke through the ice in one city fountain and wallowed in a trough of frigid water.

The Polar Bears still play water volleyball every Wednesday at noon, followed by lunch beside the 50-meter pool. But it appears the newer generation of Bears is less bold than

MerMacs (clockwise from top right) Helen Irelan, Irene Felter, Dorothy Liberty, Pat Trulsen, Margaret Maves and Catherine Foyston display the formations the synchronized swimmers use in their shows.

Don Brown was first in the water on a 40-degree New Year's Day 1955, and Orm Binford is close behind. Earl Gardner, John Zehntbauer, Giff Martin and John Greden wait their turns on the Staff Jennings dock, while spectators keep their clothes on.

the founders; frigid dips are few. However, the Bears have achieved the august stature of MAC committee.

The desire for recreational exercise gave birth to other aquatic innovations in the '50s. In late 1953, Jack Pobochenko was approached by Marie Pangborn and Freddy Benz about forming a special swimming group "for house-wives and working girls." The idea, born as the Mermaids, evolved into the MerryMacs. The group's purpose was to appeal to women who wanted less vigorous water sports than competitive swimming.

At first pegged as "fun and games in the pool," the MerryMacs' sport soon became water volleyball. The first-ever championship game was played between Nymphs and Mermaids in 1955.

The MerryMacs formed club teams each year, initially competing with women from the Aero Club and Columbia Athletic Club. But with those clubs closed, the MerryMacs started in-house teams; they have competed within the club since 1968. The added camaraderie of their own social events has made the Merry-Macs a club within a club.

Synchronized swimming first appeared at MAC in 1955, but it became part of club culture with an event two years later. In 1957, the women's showers were remodeled to include tiled, individual stalls for the first time. This was cause for celebration.

These Polar Bears stole the brown bears' pool at the Portland Zoo for their New Year's dip in 1962. They cleaned out the pool first, of course.

Betsy Austen, with help from Coach Lee Jack Powell, organized a water show to mark the occasion. Others soon clamored to join, and the Rhythmettes were born. Renamed the MerMacs, they refined water exercises to the series of strokes, stunts (called figures) and floats involved in synchronized swimming. Their success led to formation of a junior group, the MacQuamaids, in 1974. The MerMac Swimposium, in its 25th year in 1990, attracts synchronized swimmers and coaches from through-out the Northwest to learn and dis-play new techniques. Synchronized swimming was added to the 1984 Olympics as a demonstration sport.

MAC
MEMORABILIA

ONCE CALLED
RACKETS BY ITS ENGLISH
ORIGINATORS, THE SPORT
CAME TO BE KNOWN AS
SQUASH RACQUETS IN THE
MID-1800S WHEN A SOFTER
BALL BECAME VOGUE. IN THE
'30S AND '40S, MAC TENNIS
PLAYERS — RAINED OFF THE
OUTDOOR COURTS — MOVED TO
THE GYM AND TRIED SERVING
AGAINST THE WALLS. THE GAME OF
"SQUASH TENNIS" DREW ABOUT 150
MEMBERS. THE CONSTRUCTION OF
TWO REGULATION COURTS IN 1949 PUT
SQUASH RACQUETS INTO FULL STRIDE.
IN 1951, THE CLUB HELD ITS FIRST
HANDICAP EVENT AND, IN 1953, HOSTED A
REGIONAL MEN'S TOURNAMENT. THE CLUB
ADDED VENTILATION TO THE SQUASH
COURTS IN 1955, MAKING THE COURTS
BEARABLE IN THE SUMMER. THE SAME
YEAR, JUNE LEE WON THE FIRST WOMEN'S
SQUASH MEET EVER HELD ON THE
PACIFIC COAST.

fit squarely over the clubhouse and stadium. MAC plans came to a grinding halt.

The freeway was just one facet of America's torrid post-war love affair with the car. MAC members filled nearby streets to overflowing with cars parked curbside. The club's first 66-space parking lot opened in May 1951. It "will not add to the beauty of the club setting," President E.D. Smith lamented. Worse yet, the small patch soon proved insufficient. And, because new cars were so large, the clubhouse itself had to change. The old Greco-Roman porte cochere was replaced with a more accessible awning-covered driveway and entrance in 1954, to the relief of countless drivers who had sustained dents and scratches negotiating the trouble spot.

Parking emerged as a committee-level priority. The club quickly acted on all offers to buy nearby properties that would provide relief, and an asphalt apron spread south of the clubhouse. Yet, parking problems continued to provide fodder for Perry's *Winged M* columns throughout the decade.

Jeff Hockley, 3½, visits Santa at the 1952 annual Children's Christmas Party.

SOCIAL CHANGES

MAC still produced national champions, still served families, still mirrored its community. But the Depression and World War II had taken a toll on sports; social activities now stood in the spotlight.

While the President's Ball, inaugurated in 1951, and the filled-to-capacity Saturday night dances recalled bygone years, no charter member had ever dreamed of a MAC fashion show. The venerable club library was displaced by the new Crystal Room, a multi-purpose gathering spot. Dining room patronage increased geometrically. MAC conducted its first members-only charter tour to Hawaii in 1953; club travel no longer centered around athletics. Once-taboo liquor, served by the drink after 1953 changes in Oregon law, eliminated the need for liquor lockers. Though management was concerned

▶ page 114

Louise Godfrey

Verne Perry had his work cut out for him. As club manager, James Richardson was a tough act to follow — so tough that the first person hired to fill his shoes had lasted just over a year.

Perry, who came to MAC in September 1949, brought 25 years of experience in Portland-area clubs to the job. His first job out of Benson Polytechnic had been at the Multnomah Golf Club. An avid golfer, he had also managed Columbia-Edgewater and Portland Golf Club. As a manager, Perry was willing to experiment. He became known at MAC for saying, "How do we know it won't work if we don't try?"

The results of some of those "tries," or "Perry Projects," as they were called, became successful club programs, many of which endure. Though not necessarily Perry's ideas, he gave the support needed to start up the Early Birds, MerryMacs, the all-day family swim that replaced a morning father-son hour, ski schools, junior baseball, the Presidents' Ball and the opening of the body building department to women.

Perry also fostered the social side of the club. Bavarian and beef buffets, St. Patrick's Day parties and other activities were just some of the elements that led club membership to nearly double and dues revenue to nearly quadruple. When he retired, MAC had 11,700 members and 225 employees. To accommodate that growth, Perry had spearheaded construction of the club's first addition (Phase I), planning for the new clubhouse (Phase II), parking lot development and sale of the stadium. Some said Perry brought the club into the 20th century.

One of Perry's greatest assets during this time of exponential growth was Louise Godfrey. At MAC from 1938 to 1970, with a break for naval service during World War II, she worked as the manager's secretary as well as with the board and the committees whose activities were so vital to the club. During Perry's tenure she took on editorship of The Winged M, *putting it in the hands of members by the first of each month instead of halfway through. Before she retired in 1970, she capped her career by writing the history of MAC's first 75 years.*

Perry's long-planned retirement on June 1, 1970, lasted only two short months. He died unexpectedly at the end of August; The Winged M *issue that was to highlight his retirement party instead featured his obituary.*

Verne Perry

ROY DURST

Though he had left MAC to manage the stadium, James Richardson never passed up the opportunity to promote boxing. In LeRoy Durst, he saw a fine boxing coach. Durst, a Nebraska farm boy who began boxing at 19, won a six-state Midwest tournament in the '30s and fought professionally in the '40s. He came to the club on his 29th birthday in 1948 to begin a career that spanned 42 years.

Building talent through athletic memberships, Durst took teams all over the Northwest, reaching Olympic elimination matches in San Francisco and Las Vegas. Among his most successful boxers was Hugh Minsker, who attained a national reputation in the '50s. Later, Durst worked with Hugh's son Andy Minsker, an Olympic finalist, outside of MAC.

Yet, Durst's impact was most strongly felt through children's lessons. He touted the sport as a marvelous builder of self-confidence, and though he admitted his methods were sometimes strong, he believed they built character and strength of spirit.

When interest in boxing began to ebb in the late 1950s, Durst started coaching the boys' baseball team, and became advertising manager for The Winged M. *Often working 15-hour days, he also ran the Early Birds program and became Sunday manager of the club. He continued teaching boxing, bringing his gruff style to mold a new generation of young boys. And, all knew that under that tough, old-guy hide was someone who cared.*

about the cost of inventory and the temporary loss of what had been substantial locker rental fees, the increase in bar patronage soon turned a profit.

An early '50s proposal to eliminate athletic memberships prompted boardroom skirmishes against erosion in the role of club sports. President Weiss protested, "Let me first of all dispel any fear. . .that we are moving toward de-emphasis of athletics. In 1955 we had a more varied program, spent more money on this activity, and had greater member participation than any year in history. This to me does not sound like liquidation of the department." True, but he neglected to mention how youthful MAC athletes had become.

Kids, like cars, were everywhere. To anticipate their effect, the youth activities committee was formed in 1953. Juniors even had their own club telephone line. By 1959, kids decisively dominated club sports in levels of activity not seen since the '20s. A new term, age-group record, entered the vocabulary of statisticians.

Juniors played Pygmy, Pee Wee and Babe Ruth baseball, packing *Winged M* pages with team portraits. They filled MAC's swimming, archery and tennis classes. Pop Warner football returned red and white teams to the

Coach Roy Durst taught that age, size and shape are no barriers in learning defense. The long and the short and the tall were invited to use boxing room facilities.

gridiron for the first time since 1926. MAC's own ski school, begun in 1952, had 30 to 40 instructors teaching hundreds of youngsters at Mount Hood.

Among seniors, new recreational sports evolved and women's athletics gained new acceptance. Water volleyball and synchronized swimming emerged. In 1957, a group of morning exercisers persuaded reluctant management to serve breakfast as in the past. Their daybreak enthusiasm earned them the name "Early Birds." A group of homemakers, dubbed the Mermaids by *The Winged M*, competed informally against other local clubs. The conditioning department opened to women in 1953, and yielded a new facility, the "Figurette Room," in 1958.

Eating, socializing and dancing to Roger Neff's band were the popular activities on November 12, 1955, at the "Tuxedo Junction," a function attended by 350 high school members and guests.

Though no longer in the limelight, senior and junior competitors maintained MAC's legacy of champions. Swimmers continued to break records and compete internationally. Cy Mitchell restored wrestling's pre-war eminence. MAC squash and handball players emerged as national competitors. MAC boxers again dominated regional competition, advancing to national ring finals.

The dynamics of the '50s at MAC was matched by its irony. Ending the decade financially healthy and with more than 8,000 members, the need for new facilities was pressing. But once again, the determining factors were out of club control. Instead of the stadium, a proposed freeway held the key, and soon the door would open.

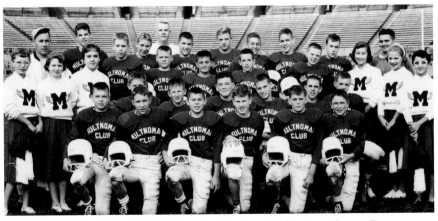

MAC's 1958 Pop Warner football team played in the parks department league. Team members were: front row, C. Anderson, M. Grosz, G. Colton, M. Ager, B. Macy, B. Heath; second row, seated, M. Boyce, B. Kaiser, S. Duden, J. McKelligon, G. Robertson, S. Stebinger Jr.; standing: B. Walsh, B. Brownridge, D. McMillan, R. Farrens Jr., S. Cress, J. Mayer, M. Groening, B. Claridge, R. Floweree, T. Lathrop, J. Harrow, S. Dawson. Cheerleaders on left, S. Jester, N. Laman, F. Krieske; on right, L. Mitchell, G. Corbett, R. Schueler. Coach Hal Ellmers is at right; his assistants, Elwin Paxson, center of back row; and Roy Durst at left.

"*If* Al hasn't taught it, it hasn't been invented," said a 1973 Winged M article on Al Tauscher, legendary MAC instructor.

Named assistant athletic director in 1923, Tauscher rose to director in 1928. But he had earlier become an athletic member in 1915, winning several wrestling trophies. He had also joined a small cadre of men who created the sport of bodybuilding by exercising with light and heavy weights. In 1916, he set a world record as the first person to lift more than twice his weight.

When World War I began, the 5-foot-4-inch Tauscher joined the Marines, only to be rejected as too short. He convinced the Marines of his strength and spent the war years doing strong-man vaudeville shows for recruiting.

Once at MAC, Tauscher set a brisk pace finding activities to suit the times. "I used an old Irish trick with activities," he once said. "When it got old I would sit on it until it died and pick up a new one." That meant teaching very little wrestling and no boxing. But he did start a course in self-defense, revived archery, introduced badminton, and had legions of tap dancers, ballroom dancers, and gymnastics enthusiasts. An expert marksman with more than 200 medals, he taught firearms courses, and even commando training.

Tauscher's mark could be seen in social and recreational events, too. His impact was felt on the father-son and mother-daughter banquets, the MAC Junior May Festival, tours and trips, and photography and craft classes. He was a legend at the annual Junior Christmas Party, where he handed out more than 400 bags of candy each year.

In 1953 Tauscher gave up directing to be a full-time instructor, and in his 80s was still teaching golf, tap dancing, archery, badminton and other sports. He marked his 50th anniversary at MAC before retiring in 1983.

Al Tauscher teaches marksmanship to boys age 11-18. Safety first and then skill was his motto. Tauscher himself won numerous marksmanship awards.

Tauscher as a Marine in Quantico, Virginia, in 1918. Here he is the fulcrum for teetering eight men, using his great strength to support all 1,587 pounds.

M A C
CHAMPIONS

While swimming still held a leading role at MAC, wrestling made a comeback in the '50s, and the decade brought new vigor to such sports as tennis, handball, squash, badminton, skiing, boxing and weightlifting.

Swimmer *Judy Cornell* started off the decade with four national records in the 100-yard breaststroke. At the 1950 national AAU senior women's indoor championship in Palm Beach, Florida, Cornell took first in the 100-yard breaststroke, setting a new American record. Named All-American by the AAU in 1951, Cornell soon left the club to swim unattached. She later returned as an athletic instructor.

A 12-year-old backstroker named *Maureen "Mo" Murphy* joined the MAC swim team in 1951. In the national AAU women's senior indoor championships in 1955, Murphy won the 200-yard backstroke title. Later that year, she was on the U.S. exhibition swim team sent to Europe and the Middle East. She was named All-American by the AAU in December 1955. Murphy won a berth on the 1956 U.S. Olympic swim team with a second-place qualifying time in the 100-meter backstroke of 1:15.2, 2/10ths of a second off the first-place finisher. She placed fifth in the Olympics in Melbourne, Australia.

MAC sent teams to national and regional contests throughout the decade. Women swimmers took four national AAU medals in Houston in April 1951, and two years later broke national records in the 600-yard and one-mile relays. MAC teams took seven straight Far Western championships, 1951-1957.

Beginning his MAC career as a boxer in the 1940s, *Nixon "Nick" Munly* soon took up weightlifting, winning his first state novice meet in 1947.

Maureen Murphy

Judy Cornell

Bill Babson

He tore through the '50s winning state and regional middleweight and light heavyweight events, including a 165-pound class title at the 1951 Pacific Northwest weightlifting and physique championships, where he also took the "Best Arms" award for his physique. He won the junior national weightlifting championship, light heavyweight division, in 1958, and in 1959 captured that division in the Pacific Coast weightlifting and physique championships. Munly continues a lifetime sports career, winning a national masters weight-lifting age-group title in 1990 and ranking as one of the top eight USTA masters tennis players in the Northwest.

In 1950, at age 17 and 112 pounds, MAC boxer *Hugh Minsker* won the state championship, the Oregon and Tacoma Golden Gloves crowns, and took a silver medal at the national championships in Boston. Known for high levels of sportsmanship, Minsker won the state title and was a national finalist in 1951 at 118 pounds. Though he was Oregon AAU champion in 1952, he lost in the semi-finals for an Olympic team berth. Later that year, he was the Canadian Diamond Belt and Tacoma Golden Gloves 125-pound champion. In 1953, he was a finalist at the national championships; in 1954 he won the state lightweight championship at the Oregon AAU tournament.

Darryl McQuarry, MAC bantamweight, won the Portland and Tacoma Golden Gloves tournaments in 1957, also taking Tacoma's annual "Golden Boy" award as "most inspirational fighter." Also in 1957, McQuarry reached the semi-finals of the AAU national championships in Boston.

MAC Olympic hopeful *C. Alan Fischer* was named as an alternate to the 1952 Olympic ski team after placing fifth in the Olympic downhill trials, but he was unable to compete because of an injury. After a successful college career at the University of Washington, he continued as a member of the MAC ski team for several years.

In squash racquets, *Emery Neale* and *Bill Babson* represented MAC on the five-man national championship team that routed a team from the U.S. Naval Academy in 1957. Neale enjoyed pointing out that on the West Coast there were just 17 squash courts, while New York City alone had 42 squash clubs. Neale and Babson also emphasized the fact that their team, average age 35, had polished off the far younger midshipmen from Annapolis. A dual sport athlete, Neale also gained notoriety in tennis throughout the 1960s.

Bob Schoning, first MAC member to reach national handball finals, took Northwest singles championships in 1949 and 1950, and finished third in the 1950 nationals. The same year, he joined *Sanford "Sandy" Wollin* to take the state doubles title. Teamed with *Bill Inglesby* in 1954, Schoning reached the quarterfinals in the national doubles championships. With *Ramsey Fendall*, he won state doubles in 1956. Schoning won the club-sponsored Northwest USHA handball championships in 1958, and also that year reached the semi-finals of the AAU national handball championships in San Francisco. By 1968, he held more than 40 first-place trophies.

Famous as one of Cody's Kids from 1938-1947, *Mary Anne Hansen Wolfe* had another sports career besides swimming: badminton, which she learned at Grant High School. In 1949 she started badminton competition for MAC, meanwhile meeting her future husband, Dr. Gordon Wolfe, on the courts. She proved to be as tenacious a competitor with a racquet as she had been in the water, taking 12 Oregon women's singles championships through 1966 and runner-up twice. She also competed on numerous state championship women's doubles and mixed doubles teams with many other club members, including *Louise Cicrich*, *Mabel Brandon*, *Helen Phillips*, *Grace Noraine*, *Nedra Thatcher* and *Claude Hockley*. President of the Oregon Badminton Association in 1960, and many times a member of MAC's Badminton Committee, she co-chaired it with her husband in 1974-75. Wolfe began participating in badminton at the masters level in the 1970s, continuing her winning ways.

The decade ended on a positive note. The Oregon Sports Hall of Fame was established, with its banquet held at MAC April 22, 1959. Four club athletes were among the original 15 inducted: *Nancy Merki*, *Louis E. Kuehn*, *H.W. "Bert" Kerrigan* and *Dan C. Kelly*.

Nick Munly

Hugh Minsker

Bob Schoning

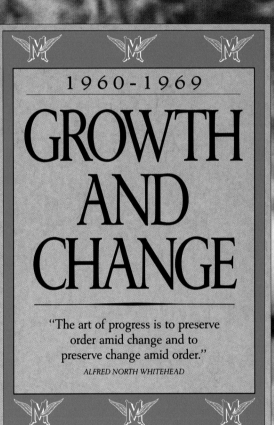

1960-1969

GROWTH AND CHANGE

"The art of progress is to preserve
order amid change and to
preserve change amid order."

ALFRED NORTH WHITEHEAD

MAC
TIMELINE

1960

RUNNER WILMA RUDOLPH WINS THREE OLYMPIC GOLDS
OREGON POPULATION 1,768,687

1961

PORTLAND TO SALEM FREEWAY COMPLETED
BERLIN WALL CONSTRUCTED

1962

MARILYN MONROE DIES
OCTOBER 12 WINDSTORM WREAKS HAVOC ON WESTERN OREGON

1963

JOHN F. KENNEDY ASSASSINATED
UNEMPLOYMENT WORST U.S. PROBLEM

1964

CALIFORNIA SURPASSES NEW YORK AS MOST POPULOUS STATE

1965

FIRST AMERICAN SPACE WALK
HOUSTON ASTRODOME IS FIRST COVERED ATHLETIC STADIUM

1966

FORTY-EIGHT HOUR CHRISTMAS TRUCE OBSERVED IN VIETNAM

1967

50,000 DEMONSTRATE AGAINST VIETNAM WAR IN WASHINGTON, D.C.
JIM RYUN SHAVES MILE TIME TO 3:51.1
BILLIE JEAN KING SWEEPS NEARLY ALL WOMEN'S TENNIS MATCHES
FIRST SUPER BOWL; GREEN BAY DEFEATS KANSAS CITY 35-10

1968

MARTIN LUTHER KING JR. ASSASSINATED
ROBERT F. KENNEDY ASSASSINATED

1969

U.S. LANDS FIRST MAN ON MOON

The Baby Boom echoed in the halls of the Salmon Street clubhouse. Three decades after creation of the family membership, family needs — particularly those of juniors — guided MAC more than ever. Club programs provided much-needed reinforcement of family values during an era of an ever-widening generation gap.

"If I can get the mothers and the children interested, the fathers are never going to drop out," Bob Johannesen predicted as assistant manager. He was right. Membership, about 8,500 in the late 1950s, increased more than 37 percent to 11,607 by the end of the '60s. Every category would close at least once during the decade. By 1968, the length of time senior families spent on the waiting list was seven to eight years.

The impact of juniors was unmistakable. In 1967 alone, 12 athletic programs were added, for a total of 28 — everything from archery to tap dancing, gymnastics to karate. Fencing was revived after a 40-year hiatus. Skiing boomed as young people discovered winter sports.

Junior members had their own social needs as well. In the early '60s, HiMacs — complete with its own board — touted programs for high school-age

Athletic instructors Joe Loprinzi, Roy Durst and Reta Denora examine cards designed to record members' progress on their individually prescribed exercise programs.

CHAPTER OPENING PHOTO: *Olympic gold medalist Carolyn Wood was met at the Portland airport by a crowd of youthful admirers and Beaverton High School classmates as well as former Olympians Maureen Murphy and Louis "Hap" Kuehn.*

members. Charm classes conducted by former Miss New York State Reta Denora tempted girls with "a complete personal study of the natural traits of charm and poise, ranging from makeup to figure to wardrobe to voice and personality."

Programs for senior members became more structured; as membership grew, so did diversity. Social programs sought not only to entertain but also to edify. In February 1963, 20 "trembling women" met to plan a series of informative programs. Lunch and Learn, as the noon series came to be called, was so well received that it spawned another group, Theater Arts Unlimited (TAU). Despite trustees' guarded reaction to a TAU request, the old Men's Bar was converted into the Little Theater. Its debut in May 1966 drew 300. A TAU offshoot, the MusicMacs dixieland combo, earned separate committee status in 1967.

In 1961, nearly 20 years after World War II halted the first attempt, a women's chorus was formed. The MelloMacs met with quick success, earning a State Department invitation to sing at the 1964 New York World's Fair.

Fencing resurfaced as a club sport in the '60s. Among these fencers are Jeff Rose, third from left, and Cheryl DeLashmutt, far right. In 1968, MAC's high school fencing team took first place in a David Douglas High School invitational tourney.

A new social distinction emerged – single adults – and MAC accommodated them, too. Single Associate Women and Seniors, or SAWS, kept members entertained with theme parties, dinners and activity-oriented outings.

Managing the myriad functions became formidable. Mel Fox was named athletic director in 1967, freeing Bob Johannesen to concentrate on management duties. By 1969, committee members totaled 277. The diversity envisioned by Manager Verne Perry years earlier had been realized.

The growing number of members – coupled with the decade's only increase in dues, in 1967 – had yielded nearly 19 percent more income to support club programs.

Jolene Thorpe delivers a side snap kick to Mark Brown as the first session of the 1968 karate class draws to a close.

ATHLETIC CLUB OR SOCIAL CLUB?

In late 1961 the board made sweeping changes in club sponsorship of members in athletic meets. Participants became responsible for more of their own travel expenses. The resulting controversy was unexpected. "Is the Multnomah Club to be an athletic club or a social club? A number of people

▶ *page 126*

As youths, Joe Loprinzi and his brother Sam saw a strongman act at the old Hippodrome Theater. The impressionable boys were so captivated they made their first weights by pouring cement into old cans and putting pipe in between. Soon, they were reading Charles Atlas brochures and scouting railroad tracks for old pipes and wheels. A lifetime involvement in weightlifting and weight training had begun.

Joe came from his home gym to the club as an athletic member in 1934, the second Loprinzi to compete for MAC (brother Gus was a boxer in 1926 and '27). Helped by the opportunity to train and compete with some travel and training expenses paid in those tough times, Joe took the state amateur title in weight-lifting in 1936. Several brothers and cousins from his large Italian family also competed under the MAC banner.

In 1937, Jack Peebler, head of the weight room and massages, wanted Loprinzi to be his assistant — and asked him to work the first three weeks free. Nego-tiating the modest salary of $60 per month plus a typewriter, Joe accepted. When Peebler left in 1940, Joe became director of men's conditioning and brought Sam in as his assistant.

Joe Loprinzi as a U.S. Navy instructor at Treasure Island in 1944.

The brothers worked together at the club until the war broke out, when they entered the Navy. "We logged 40,000 miles of sea duty and ended up as instructors at Treasure Island," where they had their own gym, Joe said later. "We were never separated."

At the top of Mount Hood in 1967 are, kneeling, Rick White, Dick Jabbs, Stewart Tremaine, David Eccles; and, standing, Robb Johannesen, Joe Loprinzi and Larry Paulus. In a stunt that was a surprise to Loprinzi, many of these members carried a weight bench and weights to a ridge and challenged Loprinzi to do a few reps.

Back from the war, they took different paths. Joe returned to the club in 1946, soon adding squash coach to his duties. Sam became the Most Muscular Man in America and was runner-up for Mr. America in 1946; he later opened a gym which still operates today.

Joe made a fine distinction between weightlifting and weight training, the first being focused on competition and the second on progressive exercises for overall fitness. While weight training gave him his entrée to MAC, he once said, "I'm a great believer in all-around exercise." His commitment to fitness became a lifelong pastime, whether he was playing basketball or baseball for personal pleasure, or developing new ways to make physical fitness fun for members. "If it's fun, they're going to come back,'' he said.

Loprinzi incorporated light weights into calisthenics and aerobics. His enthusiasm led to greater opportunities for members to get fit, as well as to the start of Loprinzi's ''Early Bird'' exercise program on KGW-TV in 1960. For 18 years he hammed it up as he got people off their couches for a morning stretch.

In 1961 Loprinzi started the club's first jogging program. His popularity and penchant for fun caused many members — the early loyalists were known as Joe's Joggers — to tag along on workouts and helped to solidify the sport's popularity at MAC. For years, members eagerly joined him on his Halloween birthday runs. He also celebrated the birthdays of his club friends by finding new challenges: Charlie Johnson recalled that for his 70th birthday, Loprinzi led a group on a run of all the stairs in the stadium.

Because he wanted to encourage fitness, Loprinzi had a hard time turning members down when they asked him to join their exercise. He frequently found himself running several times a day. ''I'd run with the members all the time and I couldn't say no.'' In his 70s, hip trouble led him to switch to walking; he was one of the first to see its advantages. ''The power of walking, to me, is very good,'' he said.

Walking was not the only area where Loprinzi forecast a fitness trend. At the encouragement of Verne Perry, he added a women's weight training and conditioning class in 1953. ''People thought that weight training with women would be

ridiculous,'' he later said. ''And I said, 'You wait. Weight training is going to be very good for women.' And I used to say the same thing about athletes. . . . All athletes will be using it.'' At first, seven women started meeting in the weight room of the old gym, but soon, that number jumped to about 100. ''We used to work with little Lady Bells, then would do calisthenics to the piano music,'' he said.

Helping and encouraging all to do their best, Loprinzi at age 75 in 1990 was still prescribing corrective exercises and taking a personal interest in their progress. Yet, while he instituted new programs that kept the club on the cutting edge in fitness, he will probably be best remembered for making it fun. In appreciation, the Joe Loprinzi Inspirational Award was established in 1988; Leland S. ''Bud'' Lewis was the first recipient.

Joe Loprinzi holds Morie Johnson over his head in a hand-balancing act at Treasure Island in 1944.

MAC
MEMORABILIA

THE MAC SKI SCHOOL, STARTED IN 1952, CONTINUED TO BE A POPULAR JUNIOR ACTIVITY IN THE '60S. A CHARTERED BUS CARRIED THE KIDS TO THE MOUNTAIN, MULTORPOR SKI BOWL PROVIDED THE INSTRUCTORS, AND IF ALL WENT WELL MOTHER NATURE BROUGHT THEM SNOW. AFTER COMPLETION OF THE CLASS, EACH PARTICIPANT WAS GIVEN A MAC SKI SCHOOL PATCH SUCH AS THE ONE SHOWN ABOVE.

THE BOXING BELT BUCKLE WAS A BIT MORE DIFFICULT TO ACQUIRE. IN ROY DURST'S BOXING CLASSES, RUN FROM 1948 TO 1990, THE YOUNG PUGILISTS ENDED EACH SESSION WITH A DISPLAY OF THEIR NEW SKILLS. THROUGH THE '60S, THE WINNERS OF THESE CHAMPIONSHIP MATCHES EMERGED WITH THE SHINY PRIZE, JUST LIKE IN THE BIG RING.

have asked this question. . . ." President Robert Hall sought to ease tensions. "It seems to me that [MAC] is both. . . ."

In 1965, when trustees created MAC's first athletic membership policy, member response was far less strident. Though such benefits were as old as the club itself, they had never been regulated. Now recipients were required to be talented athletes, complementary to club sport needs and otherwise unable to join.

Those changes signaled the decade's most obvious trend other than growth. Recreational activities, both athletic and social, led club development.

One sport did emerge in earnest. Some 45 years after MAC instructor Dr. Leslie Clough in 1917 advocated jogging as an antidote to sedentary 20th-century life, members took his advice. MAC joggers began

This young boxer protects himself from Joe Parker's left jab.

recording their distances in quarter-mile increments in June 1962. Two months later, Johannesen, then athletic director, presented a plaque to the first initiate in the 100-Mile Club, Bill Reiner.

In October 1964, MAC joggers participated in a seven-club month-long "Cross-Country Marathon," the first of many national interclub mileage

As athletic director, Bob Johannesen, at left in back, had a staff including, from left, Swim Director Jack Pobochenko, Wrestling Coach Cyril Mitchell, Competitive Swim Coach James Campbell, Instructor Joe Loprinzi, Boxing Coach Roy Durst and Instructor Al Tauscher.

accumulation contests. MAC's first women joggers appeared the next year as the sport gained national momentum. By 1967, jogging had become the club's fastest-growing sport.

SPACE REMAINS AT PREMIUM

MAC was crowded, but growth was unavoidable. Studies in the '50s and '60s offered the same prognosis. With new members, Multnomah could afford to enlarge; if it enlarged, Multnomah could accommodate new members. Once again the club sought new applicants, this time through a quiet campaign of weekly luncheons.

Welches was the site of the 1963 Women's Golf Tournament. Lady duffers included Mrs. Elon Ellis, Mrs. William J. Macy, Mrs. W.R. Lewis, Mrs. Alan Green Jr., Mrs. Bruce Mallory and Mrs. Ross Hammack.

The dream of new facilities edged toward possibility in early 1960 when the final Stadium Freeway route spared the club and stadium. MAC now had to decide: add on or relocate. For the first time, the sale of the stadium was discussed publicly. That July, Multnomah offered its property, clubhouse and all, to the city for $3.5 million.

The city was slow to act, and private sector offers were never fulfilled.

MAC trustees opted for expansion plans similar to those preferred by the 1955 board. The Salmon Street building would be replaced gradually.

A new east wing, Phase I, would be the first of a two-stage expansion plan. No mortgage was needed; it would be built with $1.6 million from the sinking fund established in the late '40s. Phase II financing would not be so simple.

In January 1964, President Franklin Drake revealed the Newberry, Roehr and Schuette architectural renderings for the new east wing. Its 120,000 square feet featured five levels with a 50-meter competition swimming pool, social swim pool, ballroom, new dining room and lounge, three elevators and increased court sports space. As *The Winged M* noted, the final plans "bore the number Z-3, indicating there were 28 revisions of the original drawings."

On December 5, 1965, 5,000 members took their first look at the completed Phase I. Athletic facilities were initiated January 16 when the Pacific

▶ *page 129*

CHEF BILLY ARNOLD

Called "Little Germany," MAC's kitchen — where up to 30 workers bantered in German — prepared some of Portland's tastiest fare.

Billy Arnold ruled this culinary kingdom. He left Germany in the '20s, arriving at MAC in 1947 after owning two restaurants. Arnold was head chef from 1953-1965, making schmorbraten, pot roast and winekraut a regular part of an otherwise American menu.

But it was as the "buffet wizard" that Arnold brought greatest acclaim to MAC. Glazed whole salmons and hams on Sundays, corned beef and cabbage on St. Patrick's Day, wurst and kraut at Oktoberfest — all this led The Oregonian to tout the club as "one of the finest dining spots in this area."

Sprechen Sie Deutsch? English-speaking workers missed a lot in Arnold's kitchen, said Bill Perry, son of club Manager Verne Perry, who worked there briefly. But Arnold got his message across. "A hot potato thrown at your back would get your attention," Bill said.

MelloMac dancer Patty Soriano and Director Bruce Kelly tease a member of the audience at the 1978 Spring Festival.

As long as she was female, any club member could join the new women's chorus started in December 1961. There were no tryouts, no auditions, no requirements except a willingness to come to rehearsals — and no name for the group. Just a year later, the MelloMacs — named by Marie Thompson in a contest — approached its initial cap of 60 members. The group had official bylaws, and the female songsters had made their first public performance at a veterans' hospital.

Hospitals, Las Vegas casinos, senior citizen homes and other locales were just the beginning of the MelloMac travels. One memorable trip took the "meandering minstrels" to the New York World's Fair in 1964, where a performance was attended by West Berlin Mayor Willy Brandt and reported in The New York Times. The group then took a train to Washington, D.C., to perform at the State Department and in the rotunda of the old Senate building.

Bruce Kelly has led the MelloMacs throughout their history. Already director of the Forest Grove Gleemen when he took on the MelloMacs, the musician/stockbroker later founded the award-winning New Oregon Singers, which became Oregon's official ambassadors of song and a favorite of Governor Tom McCall.

After a 1966 concert with the Balladeers, Kelly was no longer the only man in the MelloMacs. The women liked the sound of a mixed choir so much that they invited men to join; 13 answered the call.

In 1967, the group performed in Mexico City at the standing-room-only concert for the North American-Mexican Institute of Cultural Relations. Three choral directors from Mexico were so taken with the group's distinctive musical style that Kelly gave away his entire set of scores.

Four years later, 80 MelloMacs and "tag-alongs" flew to Hawaii, where they sang for 800 Vietnam veterans. There have been more world's fairs, too: Osaka, Japan, in 1970; Spokane, Washington, in 1974; and Vancouver, British Columbia's Expo '86.

Although MelloMac fundraisers have defrayed trip expenses, each member has always borne the main responsibility for the costs involved. In return, the club has been on the receiving end of excellent public relations, thanks to these ambassadors of song.

The 1961 MelloMacs.

Coast Squash Racquets Tournament drew 200 U.S. and Canadian competitors. MAC's 75th anniversary would be upstaged by the club's new facility.

Thanks to the sale of the stadium, planning for Phase II began immediately. MAC selected architects Wolf Zimmer Gunsul Frasca in July 1966.

Once, the sale of the stadium had seemed easy and obvious. But it actually was like the field drainage problem – lingering and difficult to solve. Now, the Willamette Valley universities had their own arenas; football was no longer a major tenant. Baseball income never reached expectations. The stadium was still a financial burden on the club, netting only $1,300 in 1965. No doubt the city would want it; though tired, it was still a civic asset.

After the initial offer in 1960, Mayor Terry Schrunk requested two years to assess the stadium matter. Subsequent political squabbles, including those spawned by other proposed arenas, ensured no action would be taken by any civic entity for years.

Robert O. Lee, right, chairman of the Portland Art Commission, and Edward H. "Ned" Look, MAC president, admire one of 26 scarlet oak trees planted around two of the club's parking lots. Trees lined the Salmon Street and Main Street and 19th Avenue sides of both lots.

As the National Football League announced expansion plans, Portland, like cities nationwide, developed Astrodome envy. Voters, however, did not agree with developers who sought public funding for their projects.

The proposed $39 million North Portland Delta Dome, the $26 million Tri-County Stadium and other contenders were condemned to sports page and barroom speculation.

Some of the 5,000 people who came to take the tour of the club's Phase I addition on December 5, 1965, admire the social pool with oohs and aahs. The Winged M wrote of "its attractive lights and glass partition to the inviting sun deck."

John Howie

THE HOWIES

Multnomah without a Howie? By the '60s few remembered a time when George or his son John had not been in charge of grounds and building. But John's retirement in 1966 brought 54 years and two generations of Howies to an end.

Coming to Multnomah in 1912, George laid out the grounds of the Salmon Street clubhouse and was supervisor when the stadium was built in 1926. When he retired in 1934, John inherited stewardship of stadium and clubhouse, doing everything from repairing balky boilers to keeping the swimming pool pristine.

John once estimated he had prepared the field for some 300 football games, until the advent of artificial turf. But the biggest headache of his career came after the 1962 Columbus Day storm, when the clubhouse was forced to close and the stadium resembled a battlefield – just hours before the Oregon State-Washington game was to begin. "I knew they meant to play it...no matter what, so we just went to work," he said then. His crew had the field ready for the 1:30 p.m. clash.

CYRIL MITCHELL

*A 1922 Thanksgiving eve smoker
began the 61-year bond between Cyril
Mitchell, wrestling and the Multnomah
Club. From age 17 to his death at 78 in
1983, Mitchell and MAC wrestling
were synonymous, through his seven
years as a competitor, 54 years as club
coach and nearly six years as a masters
athlete.*

*Mitchell took up wrestling as a
senior at Franklin High School where,
at 85 pounds, he claimed he was "the
smallest kid to ever graduate." Size did
not hold back the boy one peer called
"that little runt." A full 10 pounds
under the lowest weight category, he
entered the 95-pound class and was
soon city champion.*

*Four years later and a little heavier,
Mitchell won the 1926 AAU freestyle
championship at 118 pounds. He also
took three consecutive state AAU
opens, placed at nationals twice and
was a second alternate on the 1928
U.S. Olympic team.*   *(continued)*

At the 1964 annual meeting, a splinter group led by former trustee
Richard Lucke forced and won a vote to reconsider the stadium sale. An ad hoc
committee studied all aspects of sale or retention and submitted its findings to
the membership in "The 1965 Report." In February 1966, members voted 887
to 75 in favor of selling the stadium.

When MAC notified the city council in early 1966 of a serious prospect
for the stadium property, civic dissension quelled. If the city did not purchase
the stadium now, Portland would have no major outdoor arena. The *Journal*
advised its purchase "...to preserve some stadium facility for the Portland area
until the time is ripe to build a new one." That November, voters approved Ballot
Measure 53 to acquire Multnomah Stadium for $2.1 million, almost 20 percent
below the appraised value of the raw land alone.

A DECADE OF ACHIEVEMENT

As President Hall asserted in 1962, MAC was still very much an athlete's club, with juniors continuing to dominate competition.

MAC swimmers sustained a three-decade dynasty, reaping honors at a
pace rivaling the revered Cody Kids. Though club swimmers did not garner the
fanfare and glamor of earlier times, their accomplishments were as remarkable.
Toiling from Tacoma to Tokyo, they set U.S. records and brought home All-

*Club President Edward H. "Ned" Look and Portland Mayor Terry Schrunk sign the contract
for the sale of the stadium on December 28, 1966.*

American honors and Olympic gold. In 1965 alone, 21 MAC swimmers set national age-group records. Not all aquatic activities were competitive though. Swim Director Jack Pobochenko had long touted the pleasures of informal water sports like water volleyball and synchronized swimming. The MerMacs, once known as the Rhythmettes, held their first instructional Swimposium in spring 1967. It drew more than 50 synchronized swim enthusiasts from throughout Oregon to learn figures and strokes. Pobochenko's accidental death in 1965 only accentuated his contributions to the club. MAC's swimming influence was acknowledged by the selection of Head Coach Olive Mucha as assistant coach of the 1968 U.S. women's Olympic swim team.

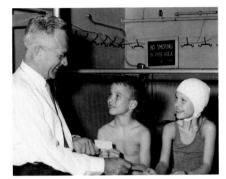

Jeff Grubb and Terry Sugg receive congratulations and American Red Cross cards after their final tests at the club pool during the summer of 1961.

MAC's wrestlers continued their legacy through the decade. They, too, would bring home national, world and Olympic championships.

Court sports became the calling for athletic adults. MAC athletes achieved national and international rankings as the new courts sparked resurgent interest in tennis, handball, squash racquets and volleyball. In 1968, MAC hosted the U.S. Volleyball Association national championships, the proving ground for U.S. Olympic team players.

MAC also recognized that amateur sports benefited from contributions other than athletic achievement. In February 1967, President Ned Look granted the first-ever President's Awards to Capt. Homer T. Shaver, Dr. J.B. Bilderback, Lou C. Coulter and Sam Lee. The new award acknowledged "the man's spirit and love of the game, [and] his companionship with and for those with whom he played...and helped in learning...."

As the '60s ended, activity and member participation remained at an all-time high. Construction of Phase II of the new clubhouse was imminent. But in December 1969, a special meeting of the membership voted to support a counterproposal to save the historic old clubhouse from planned demolition. Another study meant another delay, and once again, Multnomah would wait.

MITCHELL cont'd.

When Mitchell left competition in 1929, he stayed at the club to coach — a sideline to his insurance career. He savored the thrill of guiding teams to two national championships (1953 and 1965), as well as to 16 state and eight AAU championships. His MAC protégés included some of the top individual wrestlers in the country. In 1959, he was named trainer for the U.S. select wrestling team and traveled with the squad to Russia and Europe; he also served on wrestling's U.S. Olympic Committee and refereed in several Olympics.

For many, these would have been lifetime achievements, but at age 72 Mitchell returned to the mat. Pitted against his own age group in the masters wrestling program, he won six national championships.

The man who helped raise wrestling's national and international stature saw many changes in the sport — the advent of plastic mats, which reduced floor burns, and an evolution from brute strength to tactical finesse. He also saw wrestling dropped as a competitive MAC sport in the 1970s, yet he continued to teach club youngsters up to his death.

MAC

The wrestling dynasty of MAC Coach Cyril Mitchell spanned more than 30 years — from Virgil Cavagnaro, 1939 national heavyweight champion, to Rick Sanders.

Coach Cyril Mitchell, top center, accepts the trophy for the 1953 National AAU Wrestling Team Championship from an official. Ernie Biggs is at top right. In front, Lee Allen, Wilbur Bauer, Paul Buhler and Herb Haberlach.

Herb Haberlach, 1942 state high school champion, first wrestled for MAC in 1950, and won numerous PCI, Oregon AAU, Far West and Northwest AAU heavyweight championships in the early '50s. An alternate for the '52 Olympic team, Haberlach took part in Helsinki's Olympic ceremonies but did not compete.

Haberlach shared in an especially sweet victory, MAC's first national AAU team title, in 1953. He and *Lee Allen, Wilbur Bauer* and *Paul Buhler* did not win individual firsts, but three second-place wins were enough for the title. Haberlach later won two national masters championships in the late '70s.

Lee Allen, who began wrestling for MAC in 1952, won the national Greco-Roman title in 1954, but a broken leg kept him from defending in 1955. Winning the 1956 Far Western and Pacific Northwest titles led to that year's Olympics at Melbourne and the 1960 Olympics at Rome.

MAC pinned down a second national team title at San Francisco in 1965, with a freestyle team including *Rick Sanders, Garry Stensland* and *Gerald Konine.* The next year, MAC's team took third place in the world championships.

Garry Stensland, nine-time national heavyweight champion, won three national Greco-Roman titles, and was first in Pacific Northwest Olympic Trials in 1960, '64 and '68. In 1968 he was picked for Olympic training camp but did not make the team.

Rick Sanders, from Lincoln High School, was one of Oregon's

John Miller

finest wrestlers of all time. A three-time high school state champion, he was on the first cultural exchange to Japan. At Portland State, he was a five-time national collegiate champion.

Through MAC, Sanders engaged in national and international competition. Recognized with the 1968 Bill Hayward Award for amateur athletics, he made the U.S. world team four times, and in 1969 became the first American to take gold at the World Games. In a thrilling match, he overcame his Bulgarian opponent's 4-0 lead with a pin, despite dislocating a thumb in the process. Sanders received two Olympic silver medals, at Mexico City in 1968 and Munich in 1972. Just days after his 1972 win, Sanders, 27, died in a car-bus accident in Yugoslavia while hitchhiking through Europe.

Olympian *Henk Schenk* was another state high school champ — at 180 pounds; he also went on a Japanese exchange trip. At 220 pounds, Schenk took numerous Athletic Association of Western Universities, NAAU and USWF championships in both freestyle and Greco-Roman. He was on the Olympic Greco-Roman team in 1968 and the Olympic freestyle team in 1972. Schenk was the 1980 heavyweight masters champion.

Other MAC wrestlers distinguished themselves in the '60s. *Ed DeWitt* took two state AAU championships: a first in the 1966 Far Western wrestling meet, and a second at the 1964 Western Regional Olympic trials. *Phil Frey,*

Henk Schenk

Winning ways continued for MAC wrestlers as they captured the 1965 national team title. Team members were Garry Stensland, Gerry Konine, Don Conway, Ron Johnson, Larry Olson, Joe Casale, Rick Sanders and Grant Henjyoji, pictured with Coach Cyril Mitchell.

Emery Neale and Sam Lee

Jim Grelle

140 pounds and a high school and PAC-8 champion, went on to be four-time NAAU Greco-Roman champion and a member of the U.S. Greco-Roman team at the 1973 World Games. *John Miller,* who started in MAC's wrestling program at age 7, was part of the 1966 cultural exchange. He won an NCAA title in 1969 and an NAAU title in 1972, where he was named the meet's outstanding wrestler. Miller was regional Olympic trials champion in 1968. In 1974, while attending medical school in Dallas, Texas, he was found in his car, murdered.

In boxing, *Jerry Rehbein* was Tacoma, Oregon and Pacific Northwest Golden Gloves champion and went on to national AAU championships in 1963. Weightlifter *Fred Greco* was senior national power lift champion and national champion in 1967.

Handballer *Ted Yeamans* earned club respect for his game and for directing the junior summer instructional program.

Fred Greco is congratulated by Mel Fox upon being selected for the 1966 AAU All-American Power Lifting Team.

His second-place masters finish at the 1969 national handball tournament was the best national finish at the time by a Northwest player.

Emery Neale and *Sam Lee* went to Wimbledon three times as doubles partners in tennis, the last in 1968. Neale, ranked as the greatest tennis player ever to come from the Northwest, took 11 national titles. A major force in Oregon tennis from 1939 into the '60s, he took a record eight state singles titles and seven doubles titles. After playing such tennis greats as Bobby Riggs, Neale continued as a masters champion in the 1970s.

In 1960, *Jim Grelle* went to the Rome Olympics in the 1,500-meter run. By the end of the decade he had logged 21 sub-four-minute miles, more than any runner in history. Edged off the U.S. team for the '64 Olympics by Jim Ryun, Grelle's career included Oregon prep records for the 880, the Northern Division-mile mark and American indoor and outdoor mile records. By 1969, he had jogged 45,000 miles, and marked the achievement by joining the Early Birds at the stadium for the final two miles.

MAC swimming began another golden decade by winning seven national age-group records in 1960. The Walt Schleuter-coached women's swim team — *Carolyn Wood, Nancy Kanaby, Joan Matich, Noel Gabie, Jackie*

Danielson and *Joyce Ward*—repeated its 1960 victory in the 400-yard free-style relay and won the 1961 AAU national team title. In 1967, the team competed in meets in the Northwest, Tokyo and at the national Junior Olympics in Washington, D.C. By 1968, 17 MAC swimmers ranked in the top five in national age-group standings.

Wood, at 14, started the decade by bringing home Olympic gold in 1960, though not in the way expected. Swallowing water when she bumped a lane marker in the 100-meter butterfly, she had to drop out. But she salvaged her Olympic dreams with a stunning performance as the third leg in the freestyle relay, gaining four meters and overtaking the Australians to give the U.S. team a two-foot lead, which was extended by the anchor swimmer. The team's 4.08.9 time chopped 7.3 seconds from the Aussie world record.

In 1961, Wood and Kanaby went to Europe as members of the U.S. team. Other female swim champions were *Cathy Jamison*, named to the AAU All-American team in 1964; and *Pam MacPike*, who set a U.S. record in the 110-yard breaststroke.

Carolyn Wood

Setting a new American record of 3:51.5 in the 400-yard freestyle, the MAC team of Noel Gabie, Carolyn Wood, Joan Matich and Nancy Kanaby won that event at the 1960 national AAU championship.

The club also developed notable swimmers *Ken Webb* and *Don Schollander*. When they competed in the AAU men's swimming championships in 1963, Webb broke the indoor world record in the 1,500-meter freestyle, only to place fourth as that record was broken three more times in the meet. Schollander, at MAC from age 10 to 16, had left for Santa Clara by the time he took four gold medals at the Tokyo Olympics. He won another in the 1968 Games. By the time he was 18 he had set 17 American records, 22 world records and was in the International Swimming Hall of Fame.

Although he was not MAC-sponsored, *Kevin Freeman*—a member since childhood—distinguished himself as an equestrian. Participating in the three-day event, he was part of the 1963 gold-medal team at the Pan-American Games, where he won an individual silver. In the 1964, '68 and '72 Olympics, Freeman took team silver medals. He finished fifth individually in the Munich Games.

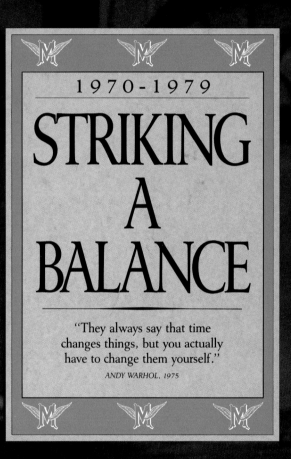

1970-1979

STRIKING A BALANCE

"They always say that time changes things, but you actually have to change them yourself."

ANDY WARHOL, 1975

MAC
TIMELINE

1970
FIRST EARTH DAY OBSERVED TO RAISE ENVIRONMENTAL AWARENESS
PORTLAND IS GRANTED NATIONAL BASKETBALL ASSOCIATION FRANCHISE

1971
WORLD FORESTRY CENTER OPENED IN PORTLAND
CIGARETTE ADS BANNED FROM TELEVISION

1972
ELEVEN OLYMPIC ATHLETES KILLED BY ARAB TERRORISTS IN MUNICH
LEAKEY AND ISAAC FIND 2.5 MILLION-YEAR-OLD HUMAN SKULL

1973
FREMONT BRIDGE CONSTRUCTED
WORLD ENERGY CRISIS DUE TO PETROLEUM SHORTAGE AND ARAB OIL EMBARGO

1974
STREAKING IS U.S. FAD
LITTLE LEAGUE BASEBALL LETS GIRLS PLAY
NIXON RESIGNS
U.S. SATELLITE TRANSMITS PHOTOS OF VENUS AND MERCURY
FIRST MAC DECATHLON

1975
SAIGON FALLS APRIL 30, ENDING THE VIETNAM WAR. A TOTAL OF 58,151 AMERICAN LIVES WERE LOST, ACCORDING TO THE DEPARTMENT OF DEFENSE

1976
JANET GUTHRIE BECOMES FIRST WOMAN DRIVER AT INDY 500
U.S. CELEBRATES BICENTENNIAL

1977
OREGON BANS AEROSOL SPRAYS
TRAIL BLAZERS WIN NBA WORLD CHAMPIONSHIPS

1979
FIRST MAN-POWERED FLIGHT ACROSS THE ENGLISH CHANNEL BY AN AMERICAN, BRYAN ALLEN

"She's a stubborn old lady," a bulldozer operator remarked. The old Salmon Street clubhouse was coming down reluctantly; nothing broke until the third strike of the wrecking ball.

Members voted enthusiastically for new facilities at the 1970 annual meeting, overruling the preservation option. On July 10, 1971, the Salmon Street doors closed for the last time after a farewell dinner dance and auction.

The blueprints for the new wing, Phase II, had long been complete, and in 1971 President Wollin quipped, "The Property Committee is holding its millionth meeting covering the past 11 years." But at $5.7 million, the building contract was $2 million more than the original budget. Construction began in earnest after the last of 491 piles was driven on January 13, 1972.

Activities and offices squeezed into the east wing, with gradual takeover of the new facilities planned. Completion was scheduled for January 1974, but the crowded confinement lasted longer than anticipated. A strike by operating

The decision to replace the 1912 clubhouse was not easy; the building held memories for many. Construction of a new facility made room for more members. By the mid-70s, MAC had nearly 4,000 new members. At the end of the decade, members numbered 16,800.

CHAPTER OPENING PHOTO: *The era of an aging dowager ended July 19, 1971, as a bull-dozer did its work on the original Salmon Street clubhouse. Destruction meant that no one would again know the secret nooks and crannies or those musty odors that identified the old club's many rooms. Excavation for the new building unearthed artifacts from the Chinese gardeners who had lived at the site 75 years earlier.*

engineers halted work for 24 days in summer 1973; carpenter and painter disputes led to further delays. Still, the National Association of Club Athletic Directors, visiting that July, called the unfinished facilities the finest in the United States.

The record turnout of 1,350 at the February 12, 1974, annual meeting gave many members their first glimpse of Phase II, opened the day before. Its 150,000 square feet on eight levels provided long-sought amenities: covered tennis courts, a new gymnasium with the state's largest indoor track, a separate juniors' entrance, 1,000 more lockers, new lounges and more dining room seating.

Removed from the 1912 Salmon Street club-house, the fireplace mantel was installed above the current club fireplace in the Reading Lounge.

It was party time. On April 27 some 6,000 members swarmed the "polished, gaily decorated palace," devouring more than 60,000 hors d'oeuvres in seven hours while enjoying entertainment and athletic exhibitions. Yet redecoration of Phase I and other details were not completed until October. Only then could the building committee conclude its 14-year tenure.

Parking still loomed as a major problem. A club shuttle van and a decade of acquiring property brought no lasting solutions. In 1979, the board authorized design of a parking facility, advising that initial proceedings were "only the tip of the iceberg."

A TIME OF TRANSITION

Sadly, Manager Verne Perry, who had promoted club expansion, did not see his vision realized. In 1970, former president Cal Souther told a retiring Perry, "Now you can start...complaining — and they can't throw you out because you're an honorary life member." Shortly after retirement, Perry died unexpectedly.

Hundreds of members govern the club through the committee system. The annual All-Committee Dinner celebrates their involvement. Milt Lankton wears a hat depicting house committee activities at the 1977 dinner.

Management responsibility passed to Bob Johannesen and his assistant Phil Wing. Johannesen's survival through years of physical and social upheaval

BUILDING COMMITTEE

When five men agreed to serve on the club's new building committee in 1960, they embarked on a 15-year journey. Earlier building committees rotated membership among past presidents. But Ralph Walstrom, chairman; Franklin Drake, Elon Ellis, Oran Robertson and Harold Phillips would stay together through the most massive construction in the club's history — an endurance record few sports teams could match.

The tasks the committee faced were many. First they managed construction of the east wing, or Phase I; next, sale of the stadium to the city. Finally came Phase II, a task complicated by financing and the displacement of club activities.

In late 1974, President Charles Haney noted the five "met every Friday over the last 728 weeks"; he compared it to two steady years of 40-hour work weeks.

The building committee toiled into 1975 to tie up the details of one of the nation's finest athletic facilities. But there was more to be done. In 1980, Robertson "re-upped" for service on the building committee for Phase III, the parking garage topped with athletic facilities. Again an outgrowth of the property committee, this group also included two past presidents, Selwyn Bingham and Thomas Wrightson, plus Ron Handel and Milt Lankton. Their work would take four years.

testified to his temperament. Like others, he was confronted with the changing mores of the day. Dress code enforcement became a challenge and a common topic for his *Winged M* column, until women's pantsuits were allowed in 1975 and men's leisure suits in 1976.

But more disturbing trends in theft and unauthorized entry frustrated management and trustees. President Charles Haney lamented, "The glow of pride…has faded somewhat with the amount of vandalism [and] theft." Activating the policy of checking membership cards in 1978 unmasked infiltrators "both young and old…[who] never had been members."

Steve Loy and Ann Kafoury were some of the 575-plus participants in the 1978 Zoo Run.

MAC also had modern tax problems – and solutions. The 1969 Tax Reform Act brought many non-profit clubs, MAC included, under IRS scrutiny. "Unrelated" income – a distinction of much debate – was taxable; an accounting nightmare loomed. The answer, though costly, was an all-charge system documenting member transactions with "mechanized bookkeeping through data processing." In 1971, a terminal with 32 kilobytes of computer memory (about 1 percent of a 1990 floppy disc) cost $7,350.

Inflation and expansion were expensive. As earlier studies had, an Arthur Young & Company report recommended adding members rather than instituting higher dues, debt, or "nuisance" service charges. Ten days before the Salmon

The Ladies' Athletic Activities Committee was in its sixth year when Sue Carlbom, Plum Snow, Jeanne Reiten, Kaye Page, Keri Nicolaisen, Patricia Bowles and Tommye Reese served in 1977.

Street clubhouse fell, the membership moratorium was lifted. In 1971, members numbered 12,183. By 1976, membership had jumped to nearly 16,000.

Membership rules were updated. Senior categories were consolidated in 1971, and questions regarding religion and nationality were deleted from new-member recommendation and reference forms. The unexpected hurdle, however, was what 1976 President Bob Mercer called "the Woman Problem."

WHAT DO WOMEN WANT?

The question was easily answered at MAC: full privileges. The Ladies' Athletic Activities Committee formed in May 1971 was not enough. Women wanted to vote at annual meetings and serve on all committees.

Divorce brought the issue to a head. With changing American values, the national divorce rate exploded. By 1970 MAC rules, a woman lost her membership if she divorced — even if she had been the original member.

A Hawaiian luau was a popular annual summer event. Enjoying themselves at the 1970 affair are Wendell Gray, Mrs. John Yerkovich, John Yerkovich and Mrs. Gray.

Changes in 1973 let divorcees remain, but women still quietly campaigned for equality in governing the club.

Initially, trustees reacted with disbelief and dismay. One told *The Oregonian* his informal survey showed "more than 90 per cent [of MAC women] couldn't care less about voting."

After a MAC women's rights group patrolled the club entrance during the 1977 annual meeting, new President William Reed called for immediate action: a committee would conduct a formal survey. Still, Reed believed, "There are as many, or more, who want to retain our present regulations as those who want to change." ▶ *page 144*

SANFORD WOLLIN

Of all MAC members, Dr. Sanford "Sandy" Wollin was perhaps happiest to see Phase II going up. President in 1971 while the construction site was a gaping pit, the Portland dentist endured months of jokes about "Wollin's cavity." The likable Wollin took the ribbing with the style he had shown on the handball court, where he and Bob Schoning won the 1950 state doubles title.

As president, Wollin expanded sports programs, discussed a parking structure and formed committees for women's athletics, doctors' health advice, dining room, publications and community service.

Wollin, who died in 1985, is most remembered for recognizing others. First to present 50-year pins to continuous senior members, he also started the Scholar-Athlete program "to promote greater rapport between the community and club." The program confers junior membership on high school sophomores, with the right to join as a regular member after graduation and no requirement to compete in club sports.

The craze took the nation by storm: rich and poor, young and old, fit and fat, men and women alike donned sneakers from the dark ages and headed out for a jog. One pacesetter for this athletic phenomenon was the Multnomah Athletic Club.

By the time jogging spread cross-country in 1970, MAC members had already logged thousands of miles and earned a wealth of experience. Joe Loprinzi had been jogging several times a day with members since 1961; his annual Halloween birthday runs had become a highlight for a small but dedicated group.

Jogger milestones had been printed in The Winged M since 1965, with runners using the honor system to report miles completed.

The Pittock Mansion Run draws men and women who enjoy the challenge of its hilly course.

An early award program had members accumulating engraved plaques, red warm-up jackets, pewter mugs and desk sets. By 1966, runners were organized into a club committee.

MAC had for several years participated in national and regional mileage accumulation contests with clubs in Oregon, Washington, California and New York. Winners were judged by number of participants, miles jogged by the entire group, and average miles per person.

Ironically, just as the sport took hold nationally, MAC's indoor track closed for construction of Phase II. Members would not run indoors at Multnomah from 1971 through 1974, when the 11-lap-per-mile track opened.

Construction could not quell enthusiasm, however, and MAC joggers headed for the hills — in fact, the program saw its greatest participation ever. The Winged M was crucial to success during this track-less time, serving as an enthusiastic booster as well as a clearinghouse for information on running events and training techniques. The magazine suggested running the "roads, trails, and paths leading up through Washington Park, the Japanese Garden, and the surrounding areas," or using

The "Original Joggers," organized in 1964, assemble for their fourth group picture. They are, front, George Hansen, Nick Munly, Joe Loprinzi, Pierre Kolisch, Jim Lafky, Bill Macy; second row, Gino Pieretti, Dr. Gordon Grout, Bud Fields, Charlie Johnson, John Burns, Dr. Collie Wheeler; third row, Ernie Mathews, Austin Matteson, Bob Leedy, Jim Carney, Ron Handel, Jack Washburn, Perry Buckendahl.

the stadium, and encouraged members to share other favorite courses by way of the magazine.

Another inducement to performance was selection of jogger of the month, which began in October 1973. Based on inspirational or personal achievement through a regimented program, one award was made to a jogger who lost 20 pounds; another to a member recovering from heart surgery.

Bob Johannesen, then athletic director, presented Lucia Warren (Powers) with a plaque in May 1965. She was the first woman to complete 50 miles.

Though some saw jogging as a "poor man's sport" that could be done in solitude with minimal equipment, MAC offered its members an alternative to "the loneliness of the long-distance runner." Encouragement, advice and recognition were the order of the day; so were challenges. As competitions came to the fore, MAC led the pack.

Sponsoring its own runs, MAC promoted jogging city-wide. First came Loprinzi's eight-mile Zoo Run and a six-mile Rose Festival Run in 1972. Later events included the gruelling Pittock Mansion Run and the MAC Mile. Members became involved in other running organizations as well, including the Oregon Road Runners Club (ORRC).

Les Smith, Portland Marathon director since 1982 and 1986 MAC president, led the race in recognizing all participants. Runner's World magazine praised the marathon, created in 1972, saying, "In Portland every finisher is treated like a champion. Among the marathons that celebrate everyone who goes the distance, there is none better than this Northwest classic."

With the indoor track open, MAC entered the 12th annual Running-Jogging Championships in 1975 — now a national event. The club placed first in total participation, with 1,276 joggers amassing 39,477 miles — an average of nearly 29 miles per participant. Club participation in the event was more than double any previous year, helping MAC beat out 21 other clubs nationally. The next year (when the conditioning and jogging committees merged) the club finished second in total participation and third in mileage. MAC runners also raised $875 for Oregon Special Olympics with a charity run. These successes and the record number of participants in club-sponsored runs led to athletic committee of the year honors in 1977.

These runners helped to celebrate Joe Loprinzi's 1967 birthday, and also put MAC ahead in the annual interclub mileage competitions. Runners include, front, Mark Smith, Marc Caplan, Scott Caplan; Charlie Johnson, Clay Meyers, Joe Loprinzi; Bob Crookham, Ron Buzzetti, Stewart Tremaine, Lucia Powers, Pete Kendall; Dick Stetson, John Burns, Mike Selleck, George Robertson, Robert MacTarnahan; Bob Turner, Millard McClung, Jim Allen, unidentified, Dave Coughlin and Garry Stensland.

While competitions spark enthusiasm, members have continued to recognize that a consistent regimen pays the long-term fitness dividends. In 1973, Dr. Paul E. Spangler and Ray Conklin became the first MAC joggers to reach the 10,000-mile mark. (This count did not include Olympian Jim Grelle, who had by this time marked more than 50,000 miles.) By the end of 1990, Conklin had passed the 85,000-mile mark.

George Spencer watches Ray Dodge's punt at the 1979 MAC Decathlon.

The survey proved him wrong. The board recanted: "After reviewing the results...the time has come to equalize membership status." On Valentine's Day 1978, women voted for the first time at the annual meeting. In another first that evening, a woman, Mary Anne Hansen Wolfe, received the President's Award.

Women gained another long-sought change in January 1980. MAC child care began for a "four-month trial period."

Despite years of upheaval, MAC social activities thrived with new diversity. Members could enjoy club-organized tours, day-trips and classes ranging from microwave cooking to pysanky. A foray into belly dancing ended with the instructor's pregnancy. Family programs expanded with Father-Daughter Day. A Social Activity Committee was formed in 1977, while familiar faces found new names. SAWS became SingleMacs; Theater Arts Unlimited (TAU) became The Arts Unlimited.

MAC renewed its commitment to Portland. The 1972 Scholar-Athlete program gave memberships to outstanding Portland public high school students who could not otherwise join. MAC scrapbooks dating from 1896 were donated to the Oregon Historical Society.

ATHLETICS FOR EVERYONE

As for athletics, "Emphasis has shifted from winning...to participating," Wollin noted in 1971. Members hiked, climbed mountains, swam rivers, rafted

Squash players in the international Lapham Cup Matches held at MAC in 1974 were, front, B. Bowen, T. McCarthy, C. McGinnis, D. Fleming-Wood, D. Kingsley, T. Vinton, D. Keefe, B. Adkisson, R. Waltman, J. Bennett; second row, H. Tregillis, E. Ballon, J. Dennis, R. Ragen, J. Scrivens, T. Wrightson, M. Jackson, J. Hutchinson, L. Harding, D. Body; third row, J. Williams, P. Green, M. Davis, E. Hobler, A. Santilli, A. McKeown, D. Radloff, D. Daly, J. Dowling; top, K. Lazelle, G. Morfitt, D. Thom, B. French, L. Barclay, T. Brucker, J. Macken, M. Smith, D. Hetherington.

white water, and scuba dived. The 1974 Ski Fair drew 2,000. Racquetball achieved committee status within a year of arrival. New indoor tennis courts arrived none too soon: 20 minutes of phone calls filled a week's reservations. Early Birds totaled 800. Members renewed the Totem Pole rivalry with the Washington Athletic Club and tested their mettle in the MAC Decathlon.

Running became an act of celebration. MAC launched the six-mile Rose Festival Run in 1972. The fourth annual eight-mile Zoo Run in 1975 was featured in print and television news; the inside of the zoo was added to the run in '79. The decade closed with the first Pittock Mansion Run and MAC Mile.

Ted Gilbert gets a time on Paul Trimble at the 1979 MAC Decathlon.

In 1972, Dick Allen was elected national director of the All-America Karate Federation. Swimmers extended MAC's legacy. Swim Coach Olive Mucha returned from her second Munich Olympics. (In 1936, she competed there; in 1972 she again coached, as she had in Mexico City in '68.)

In 1974, MAC's new gym hosted "the largest U.S. Gymnastics Federation-sanctioned meet in Portland history"; the 1975 Gymstrada played to a packed house. In 1974 the volleyball team became the first from the Northwest to win the Far Western volleyball championships; in 1975 they took second in the national AAU volleyball meet held at MAC.

Women had come a long way, getting their first Universal weight machine in 1975; 43 entered the 1979 women's decathlon. But could a late-decade novelty, aerobic dancing, be more than a fad?

Masters athletes broke the age barrier. Bob MacTarnahan earned a steeplechase world age-group record in 1975. Dr. Collister "Collie" Wheeler and Roy Webster surprised themselves and others with record swim times and All-American honors. At 76, Dr. Paul Spangler ran a world record marathon. When MAC hosted the national AAU masters wrestling tournament in 1978, Herb Haberlach and Cyril Mitchell repeated as champions.

The whirlwind decade seemed to bear out President Charles Haney's assessment of MAC as "big business." But perhaps that view was too narrow. As Mercer said, at MAC "the phrase 'something for everybody' [had] real meaning." A culture was emerging, and with it, a community.

The Totem Pole competition between MAC and the Washington Athletic Club was revived in 1970 after a 28-year slumber, and MAC regained the rights to the 8-foot statue. The battle, started in 1934, saw members competing in every sport from badminton to bridge, but MAC's Play Day replaced the event during World War II.

The 1970 retirements of stalwart employees Verne Perry and Louise Godfrey quietly signaled a changing of the guard at MAC. But most of the faces in the "new" guard were familiar ones.

New Manager Bob Johannesen started as Perry's assistant 19 years earlier and had managed the stadium prior to its sale. A year after he was hired, in 1951, he took on the responsibilities of athletic director. In that time Johannesen directed operations, social activities and served as bar manager. He knew the club inside and out. "I used to set up and show movies every Sunday here. And you could bring all your children down...while you and your husband went downstairs, played badminton, volleyball, or whatever you wanted to do."

Oregon Gov. Tom McCall is welcomed to the club by Manager Bob Johannesen. McCall spoke to members and guests at Lunch and Learn. With him is John Collins.

For Johannesen, rapport with members was helped by his own athletic talents and his reputation as a near-par golfer. He recalled working seven days a week from December to April before he became manager, since as athletic director he wanted to offer members a ski school on Sundays.

After his retirement in 1983, the hard-working Johannesen commented that he merely carried out plans and programs begun by Perry. But changes during his tenure belie his modesty. Johannesen guided MAC through dynamic, sometimes tumultuous, years of growth. The facilities, membership and number of employees all increased. Departments were specialized, bringing new professionalism to the club's managerial and administrative functions. From construction of the new wing to opening of the parking facility, from 225 employees in 1970 to 300 when he retired, to creation of several new departments, modern MAC emerged under Johannesen.

In a letter written upon Johannesen's retirement, former trustee Louis Scherzer quipped, "Bob had a quiet and effortless manner of handling matters and appeasing a new set of prima donnas every year." Chuck Haney said at a dinner honoring Johannesen that his "managerial style was performance oriented.... He was in the back all the time, but he was there."

When Johannesen moved up in 1970, MAC hired its first full-time athletic director. Mel Fox, former athletic director at McNary High School and an All-American quarterback from Linfield College, brought a take-charge attitude and charisma to MAC. After guiding the introduction of the gymnastics program, Fox became the obvious choice to succeed Johannesen.

Lorraine Miller

With Godfrey's 1970 retirement, Johannesen needed a secretary. Lorraine Miller was recommended by Fox — they had worked together at Franklin High School. Miller originally did everything from helping publish The Winged M to supervising personnel to handling minutes and correspondence for the board and many of the club's major committees.

Miller's 20 years at MAC illustrate many of the changes in club operations. Her duties began to change as booming membership led to the need for more staff support and member services. Sanford Wollin's creation of a publications committee led to creation of a new publications department and staff, with responsibility for The Winged M and other club literature. Several years later Miller turned over responsibility for personnel after she researched how to create a personnel department and then helped hire its director. Her own position shifted from secretarial to administrative.

While the club has become more professional, the friendly bond between members and staff has never dissipated. Like other employees, Miller said contact with the club's members has been one of the highlights of her career. She recalled meeting MAC masters athlete Dr. Collie Wheeler, then in his 70s, during her first week of work. Wheeler passed her going down the stairs from the third floor — walking on his hands. "That friend-

ship with Dr. Wheeler has extended all the years I've been here," she said.

Many other employees have contributed to the sustenance of that bond. Phil Wing began as a bartender in 1961. Five years later he was assistant manager. He assumed various operations functions during the 1980s and was responsible for the club's security when in 1989 he left to manage the Tualatin Country Club.

The familiar smiles of Fay Sasser and Alma Holmes greeted members from the front desk, check room or store since 1953 and 1958, respectively. Sasser's reputation for a phenomenal ability to remember members' names has carried through three generations.

The member-employee relationship was made possible largely by another remarkable aspect of MAC life, the constancy of its staff. That stability would serve to coordinate and continue club growth as it approached its second century.

Phil Wing

From behind the front desk, Alma Holmes, Fay Sasser and Lila Matthews greet those who enter the club.

MAC

John Kingery

Scott Lindberg

To be one of the world's best super-heavyweight lifters, former shotputter *Ken Patera* ''bulked up'' above 300 pounds. In his first year of competition, he won the 1969 national junior and senior titles and took second place in world championships. Fresh from four American records at 1970 nationals, he won four gold medals at the '70 Pan American Games and set three meet records. The first American to clean and jerk 500 pounds in competition, he went to the 1972 Olympics but did not medal. He later became a professional wrestler.

Joe Burleson placed second at the 1975 Pacific Coast weightlifting championships, setting Northwest teenage records in the 148-pound class.

MAC's swimming stars of the '70s included *John Kingery,* Oregon's first Junior Olympics gold medal champion in 1970. He set four records and won two other events at the '72 Oregon AAU meet. He and *David Bahler,* another top MAC swimmer, went to the 1972 Olympic Trials qualifying meet but did not make the team.

In the late '70s, swimmer *Susan Habernigg* was a finalist in three senior nationals and was ranked 10th nationally in the 100 freestyle, while *Doug Towne* held a number of Oregon records and competed in several senior nationals.

After MAC's volleyball teams won Far Western titles in 1974 and 1976, a Richard Leong-coached

Greg Kenney

team captured fourth in the '77 USVBA finals — the first time a team outside California or Hawaii had done so well. Many of the 1971 team: *Tom Becic, Dan Deurwaader, Andy Norris, John Tejada, Randy Johnson, Randy Bowles, Jack Rivenburgh* and *Craig Fergus* were still playing — and winning — at the end of the decade, as MAC took the Pacific Northwest regional title in '78 and '79.

Volleyball's *Kip Wiebusch* was cited as an honorable mention AAU All-American in 1977. He was followed by 1978 U.S. Volleyball Association team member *Scott Lindberg*, named a first team All-American in 1979.

Handball was dominated by *Jack Scrivens*, *Greg Kenney* and *Larry Vanderpool*. Scrivens, who won several state and Northwest tourneys and the 1972 U.S. Handball Association national invitational, won three consecutive national masters singles titles from 1975-'77. Vanderpool and Kenney won junior national titles before they turned 21.

At 14, *Jenny Carson* was one of just four Oregon girls to ski in the Western States championships. A year later, she went to junior nationals with the Northwest team. Her selection to the 1970 U.S. Ski Team enabled her to participate in World Cup meets in the States and Canada. Competing in Alaska, future All-American *Mary Mathews* capped the 1977-78 season by taking the junior national downhill title and third place in the junior national slalom.

MAC began a gymnastics program in 1968, and by 1971 the team of teenagers *Denise Griffith*, *Val Luce*, *Cindy Wacker*, *Terry Thornton*, *Gayle Hamilton* and *Carol Bayley* took second place in the national junior AAU championships in Florida. Thornton qualified for USGF nationals that year, while Bayley went to the national AAU Junior Olympics. Luce won a place in the first Olympic Trials at the end of 1971 and later was first all-around at the 1972 USGF Regional II championship.

Jack Scrivens

Larry Vanderpool

The 1971 MAC gymnastics team did the impossible, bringing home the second-place team trophy from junior nationals only three years after the club's gymnastics program started. Team members included Cindy Wacker, Denise Griffith, Val Luce, Terry Thornton, Gayle Hamilton and Carol Bayley.

1980-1991

A CITY
WITHIN
A CITY

"You can never plan
the future by the past."
EDMUND BURKE (1729-1797)

As MAC approached its centennial, lifestyle changes were the focus nationwide. The desire to be fit and healthy was common among all ages. More than ever before, the club was a place for lifetime participation.

By its 10th decade, MAC's total membership — almost 19,000 — made it Oregon's 15th largest town. With more than 350 members in 45 committees, its governing body was as complex, and participatory, as a small city's. The many and diverse activities guided club growth.

During the '80s, the club energetically renewed its involvement in promoting Portland's civic, social and athletic life. Late in 1981, the community involvement committee acted to enhance MAC's relationship "with our immediate neighbors and the city as a whole," including involvement with the local neighborhood organization, the Goose Hollow Foothills League (GHFL). In 1990, MAC worked to plan for westside light rail.

In 1984, committeeman Gerry Griffin proposed that MAC lead efforts to restore Hoyt Arboretum's Bristlecone Pine Trail for use by the physically or visually impaired. With advice from the National Spinal Cord Injury Association and a grant from the Fred Meyer Charitable Trust, the $47,000 project was dedicated in July 1987.

A view from the running track above the main gym shows that MAC is truly a club for all men and women, young or old. From preschool age on, members can learn what it takes to win or to lose, to share in the spirit of belonging to a team, or simply to be the best one can be.

CHAPTER OPENING PHOTO: *This watercolor rendition of the present club facilities, painted by Dennis Clemmens, is a true-to-life depiction of the MAC community entering its centennial year. The eight-story dome-roofed building on the left houses administrative offices, dining areas, banquet rooms and the Northwest's finest athletic facilities. Parking, capped with tennis courts, racquetball/handball courts, a child care center and regulation USGF gymnastics facilities, sits directly across the street.*

Gymnasts tumble at the 1987 Oregon State Games opening ceremonies as former MAC Girls' Gymnastics Coach Shawnee Ray, standing at far left of stage, looks on. The club has sponsored events for the games since its inception in 1986.

Streamers enhanced the dance routines of young girls at the opening celebration of the second annual State Games of Oregon. The games are designed to help encourage and recognize athletes of all ages.

MAC supported the first State Games of Oregon in 1986 by serving as a host site and a sponsor. Goals of the games were clear: "...personal challenge, better fitness and increased self-esteem for Oregonians of all ages and abilities." Board minutes for July 28 recommended continued involvement: "Over 1,500 children participated [in 11 sports]...." By 1989, the State Games had grown to 23 sports with 14,000 athletes.

MAC commitment to student athletes continued. After Manager Mel Fox's untimely 1984 death, a memorial scholarship was established at his alma mater, Franklin High School. The 1970 scholar-athlete program expanded to include 21 metro area high schools, not just Portland public schools.

Planning for MAC's centennial began in 1981. The centennial committee, formed in 1986, was first headed by Millard McClung, then by John Herman. Creation of the Multnomah Athletic Foundation, Inc. (MAF), in 1990, further enhanced the club's civic role. Endowed with $500,000 in corporate sponsorship, MAF would develop community athletic programs and events, aid individual athletes competing nationally and internationally, and provide scholarships. A city-wide celebration would feature five national tournaments never previously held west of Chicago.

Not all continuity, though, was so welcome; Phase II still required attention. The leaky roof wreaked havoc with fifth-floor tennis players, despite $160,000 in repairs. The indoor running track, after much debate, was rebuilt with state-of-the-art materials and rebanked to decrease the possibility of injury.

These two boys show improvement at an end-of-the-season track and field clinic meet. Juniors signed up for camps to learn anything from soccer to horseback riding.

▶ *page 156*

The retirement of Bob Johannesen in April 1983 brought the much-admired Mel Fox to the helm of MAC management. Fox,

Mel Fox

who had been athletic director for 17 years, was known as a "people motivator" who had an uncanny ability to think through member suggestions or complaints quickly and respond right away. President James Larpenteur Jr. wrote in 1984 that if Fox had one fault, "it was his insatiable desire to respond to each and every demand put upon him" by the membership.

Fox moved from athletic director to manager with ease, quickly reorganizing club programs and finances and keeping communication open between management and membership. It was expected that Fox, a lifelong athlete with a genuine understanding of the needs of the club's many types of sports, would continue MAC's tradition of long-term managers.

"There is a loyalty among the staff, and longevity with the club tends to be rather the routine than the exception," said Lorraine Miller, whom Fox recruited to MAC in 1970. But Fox's untimely death from heart trouble at the age of 54 led the club to its first national search for a manager.

That search ended just down the road at the Portland Golf Club, where Steve Tidrick had been manager for seven years. His selection in 1984 reflected the

Steve Tidrick

trustees' growing awareness of the need for administrative and executive experience in addition to club background. Like his predecessors, Tidrick would face the challenge of keeping a close-knit, family feel to MAC, both for its membership and its employees — a task made more challenging by the burgeoning numbers in both ranks.

Bob Pape

Though the club continues to grow, its undaunted sense of staff camaraderie has served to attract — and keep — many employees. Said one, "When Mr. Jo said, 'Welcome to the club,' I really felt like I belonged to a cohesive, tightly knit group. That family feeling still continues."

Many members of the MAC "family" are highly visible, and some, like waitress and bartender Penny Stapleton, have been with the club for decades. Stapleton has delighted many members with her ability to remember tastes and preferences since she came to MAC in 1949. Lauraine Prosser has been the other half of that dynamic duo since 1971.

Ray Conlon, who started as a swimming instructor in 1962 while he taught high school English, coached for more than 20

Bill Vuch

Dwayne Brantley

years before becoming early morning manager. He later used his writing and communications skills to develop club policies on emergency systems and materials safety handling policies.

Another familiar face at MAC is Athletic Director Rich Leong, who started in 1976 as gym director and volleyball coach. After leading the 1977 volleyball team to fourth place in nationals, he moved up to assistant athletic director in 1980. Leong became the department head when Fox moved to the club manager position.

Often unsung but vital to club operations are people like Dwayne Brantley, who over the course of 25 years moved up from page boy to physical plant manager. Bill Vuch, senior man in the maintenance

Richard Leong

department, has been greeting people since he started in 1951 as a busboy. Bob Pape joined his father Forrest, a member of the housekeeping staff. Bob has worked as dishwasher, busboy and now directs the employee cafeteria. Housekeeper Jackie Hill has been sprucing up MAC since 1954, holding the same shift on the cleaning crew the entire time, with a few years off for her children.

As the 1990s management team continues the quest to provide strong, capable administration for the club's diverse membership, Tidrick, Miller and Assistant Manager Virgil Kuhls meet biweekly with the athletic, personnel, food and beverage, physical plant and operations directors. All are directly connected to the club's committee system. Their goal: to be of help to members, encouraging them to use the club to their best benefit and make MAC the finest athletic and social club in North America.

1991 MAC STAFF WITH 10 YEARS OR MORE SERVICE
First Year of Employment

1937	1976
Joe Loprinzi	Richard Leong
1949	**1977**
Penny Stapleton	Whit Grindell
1951	Brigitte Blaser
Bill Vuch	Paul Hoggatt
1952	**1978**
Bob Pape	Pat Bassett
1953	Darla Erickson
Fay Sasser	Fred Isbell
1961	Slats Monson
Jackie Hill	**1979**
1962	Margaret Hilditch
Ray Conlon	Arlene Betz
1965	Jean Logerwell
Dwayne Brantley	Kris McIvor
1968	Khalid Mir
Susan Walsh	Coni Scott
1969	Sor Sok
John O'Shea	Lorinda Sprague
Charles Allen	**1980**
Ed Mitchell	Renee Ferguson
1970	Steve Harper
Lorraine Miller	Arleta Kilde
George Nelson	Ivy Ross
Anni Wurzer	Rose Snyder
1971	Ruth Sullivan
Lauraine Prosser	Buck Yoder
1972	Donna Palmer
Eloise Murphy	**1981**
1974	Skip Runkle
Tony Allen	Marge Coalman
Virgil Kuhls	Allan Higgins
Jeanne Erdmann	Bob Heim
Mary Potts	Sam Horton
1975	Sandi Hart
Barbara Boatright	Warren Chan
Don Burch	James McDonald
Elizabeth Krellner	
Becky Nelson	
Sue Roberts	

For more than 40 years, Penny Stapleton has served members drinks.

MAC
MEMORABILIA

The 1986 west end renovation project addressed the continuing need for more athletic facilities. To make room for a coed circuit training facility in the basement, the store Strings 'n' Things moved to the main level becoming The -M-porium.

The art committee continued its pursuit of an art collection "of significant and enduring value...," commissioning or purchasing works from well-known local artists Manuel Izquierdo, Lucinda Parker, Carl Morris, Henk Pander and Jude Lewis.

THE GREENING OF THE PARKING LOTS

For MAC, new construction never came easily. Some complaints greeted the temporary dues assessment required to build MAC Park, the planned five-story Salmon Street "super-block" parking facility. But obvious need, as well as neighborhood concerns, persisted. At voting time, members' ayes outnumbered nays by a narrow margin. GHFL members, fearing further loss of

During an open house, members and their guests enjoy the more intimate setting of the newly remodeled dining room. The food and beverage renovation, completed in 1989, created two more casual areas: the Sports Pub and The Cafe. The Men's Bar, which was considered aged to perfection, remained unchanged.

housing, protested the plans to the state. On November 7, 1981, construction commenced. But MAC paid a price: it agreed that a remaining parking lot would first be replaced with turf and later with at least 30 housing units.

Treasurer Dennis Ferguson told the 1982 annual meeting that due to "[the] temporary dues assessment, the prepayment of transfer fees and the cash on hand...," MAC was still debt-free. The $4.4 million MAC Park construction contract was substantially under budget. Trustees later agreed to add $2.2 million of athletic facilities to the project. On August 4, 1983, MAC Park officially opened amid celebration and exhibitions.

MAC Park boasted 540 parking spaces, three covered tennis courts, four handball/racquetball courts, a gymnastics arena and child care facilities. A skybridge connected it all to the clubhouse.

After three formal proposals and eight years of study, trustees temporarily

approved child care in 1980. A 135-family, three-morning-a-week, six-month experiment using the mezzanine-level gallery proved convincing. MAC Park became child care's permanent home. By 1986, the service had been extended to seven days a week with evening hours.

Club President Stu Hall and Portland Mayor Frank Ivancie cut the ribbon to officially open the new MAC parking and athletic facility.

SOCIAL CHANGES FILTER THROUGH CLUB

"You can allow women...just don't change the name," one member protested. In 1984, the venerable Men's Bar was the first to yield to members' new preferences. A massive $1.2 million renovation in 1989 created new restaurants; the Cafe and Sports Pub gave choices to casually dressed diners, athletes and families with children. The new, smaller formal dining room offered intimate elegance. And the Men's Bar retained its name and ambience. ▶ *page 161*

Some 2,000 MAC party-goers and neighborhood guests crowded MAC Park grand opening.

THEN AND NOW

If a time machine could carry MAC's founders from 1891 to 1991, they would be astounded.

From rented rooms at Second and Morrison streets downtown, the club outgrew four other clubhouses until the current eight-level, 550,000-square foot facility was built in phases. With its top instructors and coaches, MAC holds the key to recreational fitness or athletic achievement in no less than 24 sports. A social mecca for Portland, MAC also offers catering and dining services.

The 26 founders would find plenty of fellow members. By 1900, membership had grown to around 500; in 1990 there were some 19,000 members in all categories, with about 11,000 dues-paying.

The $75 a month clubhouse rent paid in 1891 is close to one month's dues for a senior family membership (30-older): monthly dues for 1991 are $92.50. Initiation fees, which began at $10 but quickly rose to $25, have crept to $5,000 for resident family membership, $2,500 for resident singles.

Modern members would find 1891 membership a bargain: That $25 initiation fee — more than an average weekly wage in 1891 — would have a value of $340 today, according to the Consumer Price Index. Charter members' modest investment has paid handsome returns for the club.

157

The lure was free coffee and rolls — and the opportunity to use MAC facilities early in the day, before they became crowded. On June 11, 1957, 80 men answered the call in The Winged M; by July, 66 of them had attended the three additional sessions required for charter membership. Another MAC institution was off and running.

The idea for the Early Birds came from discussions between Polar Bear Chairman George Bethell and Manager Verne Perry on ways to provide, among other things, swimming pool times for senior men. But the intent of Early Birds was never limited to one sport. From the beginning, every athletic department was involved — one member described it as "open house" at the club.

Originally, Early Birds began at 7 a.m. on Tuesdays and Thursdays only, but soon the hours were pushed back to 6:30 a.m. and then 6 a.m. Before long, Perry was providing a full breakfast at his "economy" prices — he sometimes cooked it himself — for a core group. At one point, there were even distinctions between early Early Birds, who arrived by 6 a.m.; middle Early Birds, who arrived by 6:30 a.m.; and late Early Birds, who arrived by 7 a.m. By 1990, members eager to get a jump on their day were flocking to MAC's doors starting at 5 a.m., five days of the week.

In the tradition of Polar Bears, Mello-Macs, MerryMacs and Balladeers, the Early Birds have become a "club within the club." From the beginning, Birds have had their own membership cards, with four completed morning workouts being required to qualify. Members also have their own prizes, contests and meetings. Attendance prizes have included

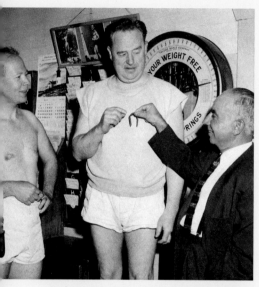

Early Bird charter members Bart Cole and Jim Powers, middle, get the worm from Fred Holcomb at the group's first meeting in June 1957.

Runners bundled up for the 1990 annual Ferguson/Murphy Beer Run. They are, at back, J. Ferguson, K. Krebs, R. Ferguson, R. Kutella, J. Colasurdo, unknown; third row, J. Anderson, M. Ferguson, J.L. Anderson, M. McKelligon, P. Cripkover, B. Savage, unknown, E. Lilly, R. Gotcher, B. Opray, R. Rittenour, unknown, M. Long; second row, D. Woods, S. Blankenship, R. Mercer, D. Ferguson, unknown, unknown; front row, L. Woodard, C. Digman, D. Rawlinson, B. Zander, B. Beall.

The Mr. Early Birds of the past gathered for this group photo in the late 1970s. They are, from left, Ralph Floberg, Pete Piluso, Dennis Ferguson, George Bothell, Lee Miesen, Budge Wright, Lew Fairchild, Tom Dugan, Neil Farnham, Richard "Dick" Allen, Jim Durkheimer and Randall Gore.

mugs, certificates and trophies, with one member receiving a live rooster and another an alarm clock so he wouldn't arrive two hours early, as once happened.

Today the Early Bird calendar, printed on a business-size card, is filled with events, from the weight loss contest which begins each January, to the Christmas breakfast in December where Mr. and Ms. Early Bird are chosen. The group has sponsored tennis clinics, runs, walks, a spring breakfast, an anniversary workout and breakfast, cycling trips, swims across the Willamette and roller skating in MAC Park — to name just some. All this activity was enough to earn the Early Birds committee status in 1963, with President Franklin Drake naming Gordon Nelson as first chairman. The group was named athletic committee of the year in 1987.

The Birds started naming a Ms. Early Bird in 1982; no one can remember when the first female Bird showed up but several recall a swimmer breaking the gender barrier.

The Early Birds are fond of stunts: once the committee offered as a door prize a trip to Mexico — via donkey. (Past president Ned Look, who won, did not go.) One recipient of the Mr. Early Bird award once wrote a list of requirements for membership, one of which was that "intellectual capacity — from shallow to brilliant — should be ignored. We must be very careful not to intrude on our memberships' constitutional right to be knot-heads."

These Early Birds made it to the top at the U.S. Bank Stair Run. Standing at back are, Marilyn Youngman, Dick Anderson, Bill Opray, Bill Zander, Neil Farnham, Sue Stonecliff, unknown; at front, Melanie Perko, Ross Mercer, Vicki Mercer, Joan Reese, Jill Buhler and John Herpers.

But behind the fun and games is a dedicated group of people who find that, when it comes to enjoying club facilities and getting an early start on fitness, the Early Bird gets the worm. From those first 80 members, more than 300 Birds check in daily.

"*I can't remember not being in the club,*" fifth-generation member Craig Honeyman confessed in 1988. For many, MAC is a family tradition. For some, the link reaches to the club's roots.

Honeyman Hardware provided early members' sporting goods. James D. Honeyman joined in 1892. His son Ronald J. served as president in 1941; grandson Ronald C. was treasurer in 1969.

MAC's "first family" is still represented by Capt. Kenneth McAlpin, grandson of the club's founding president. Three of MAC's 26 charter members were Goldsmiths; Louis J. served on the first board. A fourth joined later in 1891. The children of brothers Tom and Alan are the fifth Goldsmith generation.

The first football team's fullback W.A. Holt was club president during Teddy Roosevelt's visit. The families of Preston and John B. are fourth-generation members. A.P. Watson, the center, defected from the Bishop Scott Academy team. His many descendants include the Vial, Hall, Hall-Steinberg, Chester and Peterson families.

Halfback William B. Fletcher joined as a life member in 1895. His descendants include the families of Robert M., William L., Michael L., Robert L. Fletcher and Bryn Richardson.

Milton Rice

M. Burke Rice

Arthur Spencer

George Spencer

Amos King once owned the club and stadium sites. Descendants active today include the Littlefield and Krause families.

At no time since 1910 has MAC been without a William H. Barton, whether William I or William IV.

The Cake brothers provided legal advice to 1890s trustees. William was president in 1898. The five generations of Cake descendants include the Phillips, Mulvehill, Lash and Boring families.

A.H. "Bert" Allen, a member in 1901, played basketball for MAC and the 1905 Lewis & Clark Games championship team. The Dick and Mike Allen families continue as members.

The Kitt Hawkins family traces its MAC roots back to the 1893 membership of L.L. Hawkins, Portland park system founder. Mrs. Hawkins' father, H.A. Sargent, was club president in 1921-22-23.

Trusteeship can be a family trait. George Spencer (1988) followed his grandfather A.C. Spencer (1931-32) as president; Milton Rice (1946) and M. Burke Rice (1987) were a father-son duo. E.C. Sammons served as treasurer (1917, 1920-1926) and president (1927); E.C. Sammons Jr. was treasurer in 1975. Carl Dahl and son Joyle both served as vice president in 1948 and 1979, respectively. Carl also served as president in 1949. The Bingham brothers, Selwyn Jr. and Stuart, served as 1975 president and 1984 secretary, respectively. Karon Pittman, secretary in 1988, preceded husband Jim's 1990 trusteeship. Trustee Lourdene Graves, new in 1991, followed husband Ed, who was 1985 president.

Free cigars once enticed members to events. New awareness of tobacco's hazards prompted a 1984 ban on smoking in athletic areas. By 1989, the ban had been expanded to all areas except meeting rooms and three of four eating areas.

That same year members could enter through the front door without a jacket or tie as MAC, the casual club, emerged.

Gymnasts representing the U.S. and U.S.S.R. trained at the MAC facilities in July 1990 before competing in an exhibition at Memorial Coliseum.

Women were first honored as 50-year members in 1987. Seven of the 17 women who received their pins were, from left to right, Virginia Haseltine, Elsie Louise Murphy, Ernestine Fink, Amalie Langerman, Ilse Tuerck, Ellouise Stinson and Charlotte Gerow.

The spiraling divorce rate knotted MAC membership rules. A March 1980 change allowed members' children to bypass the waiting list for senior status, but not until 1982 could new spouses and children of divorced members be added immediately.

Rumors of marriage solely for MAC membership remained unsubstantiated.

Research completed in 1981 advised that MAC retain enough members to sustain its level of activity. To do so meant admitting new senior family members despite fears of crowding. The waiting list had become unmanageable; the trustees opted for a lottery. Success in the lottery did not guarantee membership. Instead, it placed applicants on a waiting list of predetermined size.

Almost 2,200 applied for 500 slots in the first lottery, August 6, 1982. Names were drawn at a lavish Luck-of-the-Draw Party. The next two drawings, held in 1984 and 1987, were on a smaller scale. But lotteries did not answer all membership issues. A 1981 accord with the GHFL neighbors stipulated a

A six-month experiment proved child care beneficial to the club. MAC Park was adapted to house permanent facilities.

Blaine Peters and Michael Chally try out their programming skills in a computer class for kids started in 1983.

Planning to meet demand for more weight training facilities in 1985 resulted in a new circuit training room in '86. All weight training facilities turned coed by 1990. Further expansion is contemplated for 1992 due to 1,000 more participants per week in 1991 than in 1990.

MAC instructor...Pioneer in a sport...Television exercise show host. Those accomplishments may bring Joe Loprinzi to mind, but they also apply to MAC Women's Fitness Director Susan Walsh.

Walsh, who came to MAC in 1968 after teaching physical education, says she and other MAC instructors were at the forefront of the sweaty movement now known as aerobics. By the time Jane Fonda encouraged people to "go for the burn" in the late 1970s, Walsh had been teaching aerobics at MAC for at least six years. Like Loprinzi, she combined rhythmic movement, calisthenics and stretching in continuous movements, adding upbeat contemporary music for inspiration.

During the early '80s, Walsh hosted "Bodywise," a morning exercise show on KGW-TV. Her use of men as well as women to demonstrate routines reflected the fact that MAC men were participating in aerobics in increasing numbers.

Aerobics continue in popularity both nationally and at MAC, but today's sport is different from the one Walsh helped start nearly 20 years ago. Members can choose different workouts using weights, low-impact routines and other variations. In 1990, portable steps added a new twist to the sport MAC helped develop into a popular form of exercise.

voluntary membership cap of approximately 20,000 in the year 2000. Family growth and marriage has excluded almost all other applicants. By 1990, no new lotteries were planned.

New recognition came to women. MAC launched its second century with the election of its first female president, Marilyn Lindgren. "She comes on her merits...as will many other women," President Garry Bullard announced in 1983 as Margaret "Peggy" Wood became MAC's first woman trustee. In 1984, swimmer Lavelle Stoinoff won the first Mel Fox Athlete of the Year Award. Sara Allison was elected to the board in 1987, the year that female 50-year members were honored for the first time.

In March 1987, trustee Karon Pittman proposed coordinated activities for MAC's burgeoning junior population. A May 26 resolution called "to provide a wholesome, friendly atmosphere...[and the] opportunity to develop lifelong health habits...." Junior Sports Activities was launched that

Khalid Mir

September. Within two months, Greg Barton, former three-sport college All-American and professional baseball and football player, had more than 500 kids, aged 1 to 17, involved. Some 20 percent were new to any MAC activity. By year end, their numbers exceeded 1,000.

ATHLETES IN ABUNDANCE

A 1984 ad hoc committee recommended supporting all athletic programs that members support, whether competitive or recreational. From 1-year-old Tiny Tots to 97-year-old masters, athletes filled MAC's courts, gyms and arenas. Gymnastics, with 650-plus participants, was matched by karate and its legions of followers. MAC swimmers returned to national competition.

The popularity of aerobics was apparent when Gym I became the site for a special Megaerobics class taught by Theresa Felgate. Later, the large class sessions moved to the stadium.

New athletic achievements called for recognition not afforded by the Wall of Fame's stringent requirements. The new Room of Champions featured candidates selected for their "character, ...contribution to the sport, and depth and breadth of the competition...." Masters athletes Bob MacTarnahan and Collie Wheeler plus junior handballer Greg Kenney were the first chosen.

A committed coaching staff made such activity and accomplishment possible. Squash professional Khalid Mir, former Pakistani national champion and international veteran, arrived in 1979. New to MAC in 1981, Aquatic Director Skip Runkle was named 1983 Oregon Coach of the Year and to the U.S. National Swim Team staff in 1990. Former Oregon and Washington state tennis champion Wayne Pickard was hired in 1983. Armed with the 1981 and 1983 Oregon Coach of the Year titles, Gymnastics Director Ryan Fleck also

Skip Runkle

started in 1983. In 1985, he was U.S. men's gymnastics coach at the South African Cup.

Wayne Pickard

Internationally acclaimed Sensei Junki Yoshida departed in 1990. His many champions convinced skeptics of karate's value. After racquetball professional Hank Marcus was hired in 1983, the Rose Festival Racquetball Tournament grew to be the sport's largest meet west of the Mississippi.

MAC's commitment to competition remained. The club co-hosted the United States Volleyball Association national championships in 1980. The basketball team rebounded to a 1983 Pacific Coast club title. Visits by Soviet volleyball players and gymnasts added foreign flair.

Health became a lifetime endeavor. President James Larpenteur Jr. noted, "Health awareness and enhancement programs predominate the athletic scene these days...." The wellness committee grew to become health development. Adaptive Aquatics and Marge Coalman enhanced lives altered by age or debility.

Ryan Fleck

THE PATH AHEAD

MAC's 26 founders would be amazed at the club's development. Still, as a 1990 long-range plan noted, the future holds much challenge. Can MAC remain dynamic without new blood? "Present and future community leaders... [may] be precluded from joining and contributing their talent...." Are satellite facilities the answer to expansion? What effect will westside light rail transit bring? "Old assumptions may not hold true in the 1990s."

MAC

CHAMPIONS

A century ago, they would have been famed as heroes. Few could have matched their skills or records. MAC's founders would have reacted to their accomplishments with awe and admiration. The champions of the 1980s knew no limits and their numbers were legion.

Women and juniors mirrored the evolution of squash, a MAC sport since 1893. *Ed Sloop* won the 16-and-under division of the 1982 Chivas Regal Squash Tournament. *Tony Catalan Jr.* followed him, winning the same division at the 1985 Chivas tournament. *Spencer Wall* won the 18-and-under 1981 national Boodles Junior Squash Tournament. The 1984 team captain at the U.S. Naval Academy, Wall was named All-American by the National Intercollegiate Squash Racquets Association.

Matt Rankin

Four years after learning the game, *Tricia Harding* won top honors in the 1987 U.S. Squash Racquets Association national women's B competition.

Jason Thompson, 14, continued a MAC tennis tradition begun in 1892 with his singles and doubles victories in the 1989 junior national clay court championships.

Vince Kelley, 17, used his 160 mph serve to win the 1990 national junior doubles racquetball championships.

Wheelmen of the 1890s would have cheered *Kendra Kneeland*, 1984 Scholar-Athlete chosen for the 1992 Olympic developmental cycling team during her first full season of competition.

Jack Cody would have crowed about 1980s' swimmers. *Carrie Steinseifer* won two gold medals in the 1984 Olympics. Following her victories, she thanked Ray Conlon who coached her in MAC's developmental Flying M program before she moved to California.

Jason Thompson

Tricia Harding

Teammates *Alex Stiles*, *Ryan Parker* and twins *Matt* and *Mark Rankin* surged to a national age group record in the 800-yard freestyle relay at the 1982 Junior Olympics.

Matt's 1984 victory over the U.S. record-holder in the 400-meter individual medley at the senior nationals gave MAC its first individual national title in 20 years. Later that summer, Matt, Stiles, *Jenny Shannon*, *Michelle Donahue* and *Erin King* competed in the Olympic trials. In 1985, Matt Rankin was selected as national team captain for the Tokyo Pan Pacific Championships.

Mike Miller

Michelle Donahue

Donahue and Shannon, 1983 Oregon Swimmers of the Year, also swam the globe in international competition. Donahue competed on national teams in 1983 in Russia and in 1985 in both West Germany and at the World University Games in Japan, where she was joined by Matt Rankin and Shannon. Shannon swam at the 1987 World University Games in Yugoslavia.

Breaststroker *Cristin Grant* upheld MAC aquatic tradition with her championship at the 1988 junior nationals. Ranked No. 1 nationally, backstroker *Tammy Shannon* continued a family tradition by swimming with 1989 and 1990 national teams in Europe. A 1990 Academic All-American, she set a national high school record in the 100-yard backstroke in 1991. Junior national record-holder *Brad Bachulis* returned with two golds and a silver from the 1989 Olympic Sports Festival.

MAC's century-old track and field torch was kept aflame by *Marie Davis*. The 12-year-old state champion in the 3,000-meter event struck gold at the 1990 Junior Olympics. *John Coffey* competed in events once unimaginable: 50- to 100-mile ultramarathons. In 1988, *Running Times* ranked Coffey, 33, No. 2 in the nation.

Marie Davis

"She never stops moving," one writer said of 32-year-old *Liz Downing*, two-time national champion biathlete. Ranked No. 1 in the world in the long-distance run-cycle-run event, Downing's cumulative record for 1987 through 1990 was a stunning 48 firsts and three seconds.

Team sports continued to earn club and individual honors. MAC's national volleyball team of the '80s

Jennifer Matsumura

Sue Marineau

produced three All-Americans in the open category: *Dan Deurwaarder, Scott Lindbergh* and *Aldis Berzins*, a key player on the 1984 gold medal U.S. Olympic team. MAC basketball teams stood out as champions of the 1986 and 1987 national athletic club tournaments.

MAC's 1890s Sawdust Brothers were said to rival vaudeville's best acrobats. Their modern counterparts were also impressive: from 1983 to 1990, MAC sent between three and seven gymnasts to the national championships each year.

Mike Miller, 16, brought home Oregon's first national gymnastics title in 1985 with 19.8 points out of a possible 20 on the still rings and took third all-around in the Class I (boys 16-18) division at the Junior Olympics. His first national still rings medal, a silver, came at the 1983 Junior Olympics. *Michelle Sandoz*, a former Puerto Rican champion, scored 9.55 to win a silver medal on the balance beam at the 1990 Junior Olympics.

Cameron Pittman

Few could match *Jennifer Matsumura*, two-sport athlete and concert violinist with a 4.0 grade average. Three-time MAC Gymnast of the Year, Matsumura was most honored for karate. In 1984, she and *Janet Lucas* were MAC's first two AAU junior nationals entries. Matsumura won her first national gold in 1985 for junior girls' kata (movement demonstration). She won additional national gold in 1986 in intermediate kata. Matsumura, 18, received the Mel Fox Award in 1987.

But Matsumura was not MAC's only prodigy. *Shawn Hancock*, a black belt at age 11, won his first gold for kumite (sparring) in the 13-year-old division at the 1985 junior nationals. By 1988, Hancock had won two more national gold medals and was named to the USAKF National Team. That year he also competed in Yugoslavia and won more gold at the Ryobu-Kai International Tournament in Japan.

David Sachtler won the 1988 USAKF 9-year-old national kumite championship and took first place at the Hayashi Ha Shito Ryo-Kai USA Championships in the 8-9 age group. Another karate kid, 11-year-old *Cameron Pittman*, brought gold home from the 1989 Junior Olympics for both kata and kumite. *Alex Bay*, 18, won silver in kumite at that same tourney.

David Sachtler

Karate's success led *The Winged M* to comment, "At the club, karate has come to signify confidence, self-discipline and close friendships." Many credit the program's development to athlete and '82-'83 chairman *Greg Specht*.

Specht flirted with a national championship as a green belt in 1982, before losing to teammate *Brian Lessler* at the Ryobu-Kai National Karate Tournament.

Alan Takahashi

Specht anticipated the 1985 AAU nationals remarking, "The benefits are not how one does in tournaments or promotions, but how one develops individually." After winning a silver medal in advanced senior kumite, his competitive urge was still apparent: "Second place is nice, but it's not quite the same." Specht reached national gold in 1986.

The '85 tournament, overall, proved a stunning success for MAC. Its athletes returned with 17 medals,

Brad Marineau, left, and Mark Heyerdahl

including seven gold and three silver. In his first national tournament, *Alan Takahashi* took silver in senior men's novice kumite and gold in senior men's intermediate kata. *Chol-Kyu "Kent" Kim* won his first of four gold medals in kata. *Brad Marineau* recovered from an early loss to win gold in men's advanced open weight kumite and a place on MAC's Wall of Fame. Not to be outdone, *Susan Marineau*, Brad's wife, captured two gold medals in that same meet — her first major tournament — in intermediate kata and kumite.

Brad's gold was the culmination of years of competition. His silver in black belt kumite at the 1984 AAU nationals won him a berth on a U.S. team competing in Holland and Yugoslavia. In 1986 he wore the gei of the U.S. karate team at the world championships.

Joining him on both occasions was *Mark Heyerdahl*, MAC's first national karate champion. After winning the gold in men's advanced weapons kata at the 1984 championships, Heyerdahl was selected to compete against the Republic of China team.

Greg Specht

Shawn Hancock

Mike Heffernan

Bob Hunter

Dave Steinberg

Older competitors earned a dignified name: masters. The first masters event, a 1970 Amarillo swim meet, was organized by former member *Dr. Ransom Arthur.* Fitness and fellowship, he felt, kept participants "excited, enthusiastic and motivated...."

Hazel Bressie, Don Stevenson, Roy Webster and Collie Wheeler.

Swimmer *Lavelle Stoinoff* exemplified such qualities, training just to break records. Stoinoff set marks in every competitive stroke with 14 national and eight world records. She held the national title for the "One Hour Swim" from 1984 to 1988.

Masters' interests were many. *Randy Bowles* and *John Tejada* were named volleyball All-Americans. Hardball squash national B champ in 1984, *Marjin Wall* reached the 1990 softball squash 35-and-over national finals unbeaten before settling for second. *Tom Levak* won the 45-and-older advanced men's kumite at the 1988 national karate meet.

In 1981, *Hazel Bressie*, 72, and *B. Mary Inkster*, 52, became the first women placed in the Room of Champions: Bressie for national swimming marks, Inkster for national and international skiing titles. Skier *Doris Martin* won her first national races in 1989 at age 60.

Swimmers but not racers, the MerMacs dazzled at the 1990 Masters National Synchronized Swimming Championships. Gold medalists included: *Linda Pollock*, solo; *Pat Trulsen* and *Gerry Martin*, figures; and *Irene Felter, Liz Mayer* and Martin, trio. Team silver honors went to *Marge Allen, Betsy Austen, Lois Duvall, Mary Hulme, Jane Moore* and *Jeanne Steed*.

Roy Webster began competitive swimming in 1971 at age 70. Webster swam solo across the Columbia River at Hood River on Labor Day from 1942 to 1966; after the event became public he continued until 1985. Webster won three national gold medals, and at the 1984 New Zealand world championships took six golds and five silvers.

Seven MAC swimmers joined him in New Zealand; *Don Stevenson* returned with four golds and a silver. Webster praised the oldest athlete there, *Dr. Collister Wheeler*, 91, calling him "a marvel and still my inspiration."

Robert MacTarnahan

Wheeler first participated in MAC sports in 1912. But not until 1976 did he set his first world records — three at his first meet. Of his 31 world records in track and field, weightlifting and swimming, Wheeler says his most memorable was his 220-yard dash win at age 90 over a former professional athlete.

Multi-sport athlete *Bob MacTarnahan* competed from Sweden to China, setting world records in the 3,000-meter steeplechase, the 5,000-meter and the mile. He also won four national individual and team wrestling titles.

MAC's gold medal wrestling teams dominated national meets until disbanding in 1983. Team and individual medalists were *Joe Casale, Herb Haberlach, Charles Hinds, Cy Mitchell, Frank Nichols, Larry Olsen, Henk Schenk, Bob Smith* and *Garry Stensland*.

Lavelle Stoinoff

Mike Heffernan, 45, made his mark with wins in the 5,000-meter and 10,000-meter events at The Athletic Congress '85 national games, repeating in 1988. That year, *Robert C. Hunter* struck gold in the 20-pound weight throw and shotput at the indoor nationals.

Handball players were undeniably durable. *Dick Brouwer* won national titles in 1982 and 1987. By 1986, 70-year-old *Lee Shinn* had accumulated five national firsts and three seconds in a nine-year span. He and *Bill Schlauch* took doubles silver in '84 and '86. Schlauch, 62, won singles silver in the 1986 super masters nationals. In 1985, *Gib Gilmore* captured USHA Four Wall Championships 35-and-over gold. Hardy competitor *Ed Grossenbacher*, 48, won the 1986 masters world championship. *Dave Steinberg*, the 1988 and 1989 USHA open singles titlist, took second in the 1990 USHA 35-and-over doubles with *Doug Mull*.

Gib Gilmore

Lee Shinn

Dick Brouwer

"There are only two
lasting bequests we can hope to
give our children. One of these
is roots, the other wings."

HODDING CARTER

APPENDIX

PRESIDENTS

1891 A.B. McAlpin
1892 A.E. Mackay
1893 A.B. McAlpin
1894 Edward Cookingham
1895 Herbert E. Judge
1896 Rodney L. Glisan
1897 Guy G. Willis
1898 W.M. Cake
1899 J.N. Teal
1900 W.M. Cake
1901 F.A. Nitchy
1902 F.A. Nitchy (resigned)
        W.M. Cake (completed term)
1903 R.F. Prael
1904 Dan J. Moore
1905 W.H. Chapin
1906 George W. Simons
1907 George W. McMillan
1908 George W. McMillan
1909 James F. Ewing
1910 Walter A. Holt
1911 Walter A. Holt
1912 Allan M. Ellsworth
1913 George W. Simons
1914 R.W. Wilbur
1915 R.W. Wilbur
1916 Allan M. Ellsworth
1917 W.W. Banks
1918 W.W. Banks
1919 W.W. Banks
1920 C. Henri Labbe
1921 Henry A. Sargent
1922 Henry A. Sargent
1923 Henry A. Sargent
1924 Plowden Stott
1925 John A. Laing
1926 John A. Laing
1927 Edward C. Sammons
1928 Frank E. Watkins
1929 Frank E. Watkins
1930 T. Morris Dunne
1931 Arthur C. Spencer
1932 Arthur C. Spencer
1933 C.B. Stephenson
1934 Lloyd R. Smith
1935 George Black Jr.
1936 Zina A. Wise
1937 Donald H. Bates
1938 Calvin N. Souther
1939 Herman G. Green
1940 R.R. Adams
1941 Ronald J. Honeyman
1942 Dudley Clark
1943 Ferry Smith
1944 Robert T. Mautz

1945 William J. Collins
1946 Milton W. Rice
1947 Sidney F. Woodbury
1948 Milo K. McIver
1949 Carl A. Dahl
1950 E.D. Smith Jr.
1951 N. Thomas Stoddard
1952 Henry E. Baldridge
1953 George Halling
1954 James G. Swindells
1955 Harold A. Weiss
1956 Mel Goodin
1957 Thaddeus B. Bruno
1958 Harvey S. Benson
1959 William W. Jewett
1960 Harold M. Phillips
1961 Robert M. Hall
1962 Elon E. Ellis
1963 Franklin G. Drake
1964 Samuel Lee
1965 Frank E. Nash
1966 Edward H. Look
1967 H. Stewart Tremaine
1968 William Dale
1969 Robert A. Liberty
1970 John L. Schwabe
1971 Dr. Sanford Wollin
1972 John J. Higgins
1973 Thomas Wrightson
1974 Charles E. Haney
1975 Selwyn Bingham Jr.
1976 Robert E. Mercer
1977 William R. Reed
1978 Ronald K. Ragen
1979 William H. Schlauch
1980 Philip F. Brown
1981 Kenneth M. Judd
1982 Garry R. Bullard
1983 Stuart A. Hall
1984 James A. Larpenteur Jr.
1985 D. Edward Graves
1986 Lester V. Smith
1987 M. Burke Rice
1988 George C. Spencer
1989 Dennis P. Rawlinson
1990 Kenneth D. Stephens
1991 Marilyn Lindgren

PRESIDENT'S AWARD

1967 Dr. J. B. Bilderback
        Lewis C. Coulter
        Samuel Lee
        Captain Homer T. Shaver
1968 Richard Sundeleaf
        Aubrey Watzek

1969 Harry Davies
        Joe Hammer
1970 William P. Sherman
        Collister M. Wheeler
1971 John B. Harding
1973 John Carney
        Claude Hockley
        Robert MacTarnahan
        John Scott
1974 Norman Lewis
1975 William P. Hutchison
1976 Thomas Wrightson
1977 Jack Rivenburgh Jr.
        Roy Webster
1978 Mary Anne Wolfe
1979 Neil Farnham
1980 Nello J. Vanelli
1981 Jack Scrivens
1982 John Helmer Jr.
1983 Philip Brown
1984 Lee Shinn
1985 Dennis Ferguson
1986 Hazel Bressie
        Bill Schlauch
1987 Charlie Gray
        Jim Harding Jr.
        Charlie Johnson
1988 Betsy Austen
        Tom Becic Sr.
1990 Roger Jensen
        Bob Mercer
        Doreen Morris
1991 Fred Schumacher

McALPIN AWARD

1991 Jeff Gudman

MEL FOX AMATEUR ATHLETE OF THE YEAR

1984 Lavelle Stoinoff
1985 Michelle Donahue
1986 Jennifer Matsumura
1987 Mike Heffernan
1988 Jeff Larson
1989 Brad Bachulis
1990 Tammy Shannon

JOE LOPRINZI INSPIRATIONAL AWARD

1988 Bud Lewis
1989 Mike Falkenstein
1990 George Meyer

MAC WALL OF FAME

Lee Allen – Wrestling
Bill Babson – Squash
Sam Bellah – Track & Field
Virgil Cavagnaro – Wrestling
John Cebula – Handball
Judy Cornell – Swimming
Constance Meyer Dressler – Diving
Edgar Frank – Wrestling
Alfred C. Gilbert – Track & Field
Walter Goss – Tennis
Herbert Greenland – Wrestling
Jim Grelle – Track & Field
Virgil Hamlin – Wrestling
Martin Hawkins – Track & Field
Herb Haberlach – Wrestling
Brenda Helser – Swimming
Helen Hicks – Diving
Russ Hill – Badminton
Herbert Hutton – Wrestling
Ted Jensen – Handball
Ernie Johnson – Handball
Dan Kelly – Track & Field
H.W. "Bert" Kerrigan – Track & Field
Louis "Hap" Kuehn – Diving
Sam Lee – Tennis
Nancy Merki Lees – Swimming
Don Lewis – Handball
Brad Marineau – Karate
John Miller – Wrestling
Cyril Mitchell – Wrestling
Edward E. Morgan – Track & Field,
    Football, Baseball
Tommy Moyer – Boxing
Maureen Murphy – Swimming
Emery Neale – Tennis
Phil Neer – Tennis
Chester Newton – Wrestling
Ken Patera – Weightlifting
Thelma Payne – Diving
Gino Quilici – Weightlifting
Robin Reed – Wrestling
Rick Sanders – Wrestling
Henk Schenk – Wrestling
Bob Schoning – Handball
Jack Scrivens – Handball
Joseph Harker Smith – Track & Field,
    Baseball, Football
Forrest C. Smithson – Track & Field
Garry Stensland – Wrestling
Arne Sundberg – Weightlifting
Brandt Wickersham – Tennis
Mary Anne Wolfe – Badminton
Carolyn Wood – Swimming
Suzanne Zimmerman – Swimming

ROOM OF CHAMPIONS

Brad Bachulis–Swimming
Hazel Bressie–Swimming
Dick Brouwer–Handball
Gib Gilmore–Handball
Mary Mathews Guneisch–Skiing
Tricia Harding–Squash
Mike Heffernan–Running
Bob Hunter–Track & Field
B. Mary Inkster–Skiing
Greg Kenney–Handball
Tom Levak–Karate
Robert MacTarnahan–Track & Field,
    Wrestling
Sue Marineau–Karate
Doris Martin–Skiing
Jennifer Matsumura–Karate
Mike Miller–Gymnastics
Nick Munly–Weightlifting
J. Cameron Pittman–Karate
David Sachtler–Karate
Lee Shinn–Handball
Greg Specht–Karate
Lavelle Stoinoff–Swimming
Alan Takahashi–Karate
Roy Webster–Swimming
Collister Wheeler–Swimming

50-YEAR MEMBERS

1971
Dr. T. Rex Baldwin
Charles S. Barton
R.M. Bodley
Stanley N. Boquist
James D. Brady
Henry F. Cabell
Harold H. Cake
Ralph H. Cake
Dr. Howard E. Carruth
L.R. Centro
H.C. Charlton
Gordon Clark
Wayne W. Coe
William J. Collins
Russell M. Colwell
P.W. Cookingham
H.B. Cooper Sr.
Anson S. Frohman
Dr. Oliver G. Garrett
William A. Haseltine
Eric V. Hauser
James Hefty
R.J. Honeyman
Isaac D. Hunt
Clifford T. Johnson
Dr. Noble W. Jones

Jacob G. Kamm
Dr. Russell H. Kaufman
C.P. Keyser
W.A. King
G.A. Kingsley
Robert Krohn
Louis E. Kuehn
A.J. Lampert
Duane C. Lawrence
Leon N. Lefevre
W.J. Lewis
Colin Livingstone
C.E. Lomax
Hall S. Lusk
Oscar R. Miller
A.L. Mills Jr.
Joseph A. Minott
Hobart Mitchell
Walter K. Moffett
Richard G. Montgomery
Ben W. Newell
R.H. Noyes Sr.
W.J. O'Donnell
A.M. O'Hanlon
E.K. Oppenheimer
E.L. Ordeman
Robin Reed
Edward C. Sammons
John D. Scott
Homer T. Shaver
K.L. Tamiesie
John K. Tuerck
Henry R. Wakeman
William S. Walter
Ray C. Watkins
Aubrey R. Watzek
Dykeman White

1973
Donald H. Bates
Holt Berni
F.S. Burt
George Hartness
Dr. Blair Holcomb
Frank Mihnos
Lyle C. Rogers
Arthur H. Scheufler
C.B. Stephenson
Richard B. Stinson

1974
George Friede
Dr. Charles H. Manlove
Alexander H. Sargent
Peter A. Schwabe
C.R. Zehntbauer

1975
Harry S. Coleman
Ivan F. Phipps
E.D. Wiley

1976
E.C. Curtis
James C. Dezendorf
Cord Sengstake Jr.
Dr. Collister Wheeler

1977
Frederick G. White

1978
Irwin S. Adams
George Black Jr.
Ralph L. Davis
Bert S. Gooding
George R. Merriam

1979
William R. Brown
Dr. John H. LaBadie
Dr. Merl L. Margason
Ursel C. Narver
Calvin N. Souther

1980
Roscoe C. Nelson
Oscar P. Pederson
John D. Simon
I.D. Wood

1981
Robert W. Cowlin
John H. Huber
Edward King
Dr. George D. Votaw
John B. Yeon

1982
Paul D. Hunt
Stuart Kerr
Richard Sundeleaf

1983
Haskell C. Carter
E.W. Eggen
Burdette Erickson
Harold S. Hirsch
Newton Langerman
Harold F. Leonard
Raymond J. Richen

1984
James N. McDowell
Walden Stout

1985
Glenn Bechtold
Frank M. Fink
Fred R. Fisher
Francis I. Smith
Arthur E. Watson

1986
Francis Andrews
Robert K. Bronson
C.R. Glennon
Robert E. Hodges
Samuel Lee
Omar C. Palmer
George E. Robinson

1987
Albert Bullier
Marion Bullier
Marguerite Doherty
Ernestine Fink
Lewis M. Fox
Elise Freed
Charlotte Gerow
Mildred J. Gooding
Virginia A. Haseltine
Alice M. Kerr
Amalie Langerman
Ruth Lawrence
Robert M. MacTarnahan
Donald R. Munro Jr.
Elsie Murphy
Dr. Thomas S. Saunders
Catherine Stephenson
Ellouise M. Stinson
Mildred Sundeleaf
Ilse Tuerck
Dora Walker
Fredrick J. Whittlesey Jr.
Robert J. Wilhelm
Winifred Zehntbauer

1988
Robert C. Hunter
Dr. Russell L. Johnsrud
George C. Kotchik
Omar J. Noles
Irma Pederson
Edna I. Reiner
Erskine B. Wood

1989
Alice Alexander
Lyle Ashcraft
Carol Beggs
Madeline Boone

R.R. Bullivant
Louise Bullivant
John Carney Jr.
Lela May Cohen
Henry F. Eder
Joe Gard
Glenna V. Kneeland
Charles P. Libby
C.I. Meyers
Marian Meyers
Thomas P. Moyer Sr.
Constance Palmer
Howard B. Patterson
Robert B. Riscoe
Joseph M. Roberts
James P. Stewart

1990
May Ahern
Grace Bell
Maurie D. Clark
Leslie F. Clarke
Harry M. Euler
Bernice H. Greene
Folger Johnson Jr.
Richard Lucke
Mildred Mautz
Don B. McCormick
Stanley O. Norman
Nadine K. Robinson
Grant F. Thuemmel

1991
William B. Boone
Thaddeus B. Bruno Sr.
Al Disdero
Mina Disdero
Dorothy Gary
Thelma Hagan
Eleanor M. Hunt
Ida M. Kleist
Virginia Stoll Lord
Eleanor Middleton
Sarah Miller
William E. Morgan
Claude Palmer
Helen Palmer
Alec Runciman
Dorothy Rybke
R. Robert Smith Jr.
Flossie Snider
Helmer Sundt
Margaret Wiswall

BIBLIOGRAPHY

Barnes and Noble Book of Quotations. Robert I. Fitzhenry, editor; Harper and Row, 1927.

The Complete Book of the Olympics. David Wallechinsky, Penguin Books, 1988.

The Concise Columbia Dictionary of Quotations. Robert Andrews, Columbia University Press, 1987.

Eighty Years of Oregon Wrestling: A History of the Oregon Open Championships. Michael R. Ives, Reproduction work by Chester Lund, 1985.

The Encyclopedia of American Facts and Dates. Gorton Carruth and Associates, editors; 4th edition, Thomas Y. Crowell Company, 1966.

Football. Earl Schenk Miers, Grossett and Dunlap Inc., 1967.

Going the Distance – the Portland Marathon. Nadine Wooley, Friends of the Portland Marathon, 1990.

The Great American Sports Book. George Gipe, Doubleday Dolphin, 1978.

The Growth of a City. E. Kimbark MacColl, The Georgian Press, 1979.

The Harper Book of American Quotations. Gorton Carruth and Eugene Ehrlich, Harper and Row, 1988.

A History of the Multnomah Amateur Athletic Club. Louise R. Godfrey, Multnomah Athletic Club, 1967.

The History of American Football. Allison Danzig, Prentice-Hall Inc., 1956.

Information Please Almanac. Otto Johnson, executive editor; Houghton Mifflin Company, 1989.

Merchants, Money and Power. E. Kimbark MacColl, The Georgian Press, 1988.

My Favorite Quotations. Norman Vincent Peale, K. S. Giniger Co., 1990.

Oregon: A Chronology and Documentary Handbook, Robert I. Vexler, state editor; Oceana Publishing, 1978.

The Oregon Wrestling Record and Biographical Dictionary. Michael R. Ives, production work by Chet Lund, 1988.

Photohistory of the 20th Century. Jonathan Grimwood, Blanford Press, 1986.

Portland: A Pictorial History. Harry Stein, Kathleen Ryan and Mark Beach, Donning Co., 1980.

Portland Blue Book. R. L. Polk, R. L. Polk and Co., 1901.

Portland Names and Neighborhoods: Their Historic Origins. Eugene Snyder, Binford and Mort, 1979.

The Shaping of a City. E. Kimbark MacColl, The Georgian Press, 1976.

The Timetables of History: A Horizontal Linkage of People and Events. Bernard Grun, Simon and Schuster, Inc., 1975.

United States Olympic Book. Asa S. Bushnell and Arthur G. Lentz, editors; The United States Olympic Committee, 1964.

United States 1956 Olympic Book. Asa S. Bushnell and Arthur G. Lentz, editors; United States Olympic Association Inc., 1957.

Uphill Downhill Yamhill, The Evolution of the Yamhill Historic District. John M. Tess, self-published by John M. Tess, 1977.

NEWSPAPERS/MAGAZINES

Oregon Journal
The Oregonian
The Telegram
This Week Magazine
Willamette Week
The Winged M Bulletin
The Winged M Chat
The Winged M

SCRAPBOOKS

Early Birds
Meredith Fisher
Oliver King Jeffery
Tom Louttit
MAC
MelloMacs
MerMacs
Polar Bears
Frank Watkins
Mary Anne Wolfe

MAC ORAL HISTORIES

Interviews by Shirley Tanzer
Transcribed by Marti Banegas

CONTRIBUTING PHOTOGRAPHERS

Hugh Ackroyd
Herb Alden
Leonard Bacon
Jean Connolly
Kristin Finnegan
Gladys Gilbert
Hass-Schreiner Photo
Roger Jensen
Alfred A. Monner
Les T. Ordeman
Beth Rasgorshek
Carl E. Vermilya
Ralph Vincent

PHOTOGRAPHS COURTESY OF:

Mary Cavagnaro
Michael Ives
Joel Krause
Martha Littlefield
MAC Collection/*Winged M* archives
MerMac scrapbook
Oregon Historical Society
   #cn 17901
   #cn 022210
   #OrHi 11988-9
   #OrHi 5565
   #cn 12041
   #OrHi 25592
   #cn 14214
Pacific University archives
PhotoArt Commercial Studios
Polar Bear scrapbook
Mrs. Henk (Sally) Schenk
Al Tauscher
Mary Anne Wolfe

OBJECTS LOANED FOR PHOTOGRAPHY BY:

Esther S. "Sunny" Anderson
Adelbert Clostermann
Oregon Sports Hall of Fame
Joe Parker
Dr. R.L. Rennick
O.B. and Margery Robertson
Mary Anne Wolfe
Carolyn Wood

PHOTO IDENTITIES

Pages 8-9: Squash players Dave Zier and Sandy "Great Legs" Koski; Nick Munly, Jeanette D'Amico with Joe Loprinzi and others in the weight room.

Pages 12-13: Susan Walsh and Paul Irvin with Marilyn Grunbaum, Carlos Rivera, both Greg Marshalls, Holly Barton, Kathy Wentworth and others.

Pages 170-171: Swimmers Doreen Morris and her grandson Alex Pullen.

Pages 172-173: Gymnast Mike Cook.

MULTNOMAH ATHLETIC CLUB OLYMPIANS

H. W. "Bert" Kerrigan, 1906, High Jump, Bronze

Sam Bellah, 1908, Pole Vault, 6th; 1912, Pole Vault, 7th

A.C. Gilbert, 1908, Pole Vault, Gold (tie)

Dan Kelly, 1908, Long Jump, Silver

Forrest Smithson, 1908, 110-meter Hurdles, Gold

Martin Hawkins, 1912, 110-meter Hurdles, Bronze

Walter McClure, 1912, 1500 meters, did not place

George Philbrook, 1912, Shot Put, 5th; Discus, 7th; Decathlon, did not finish

David Fall, 1920, Diving, did not place

Louis J. Balbach, 1920, Diving, Bronze

Louis E. Kuehn, 1920, Diving, Gold

Constance Meyer, 1920, Diving, did not compete

Johnny Murphy, 1920, High Jump, 5th

Thelma Payne, 1920, Diving, Bronze

Augustus "Gus" Pope, 1920, Discus, Bronze

Norman Ross, 1920, 400-meter Freestyle, Gold; 1500-meter Freestyle, Gold; 4x200 Freestyle Relay, Gold; 100-meter Freestyle, 4th

Chester Newton, 1924, Wrestling Featherweight, Silver

Robin Reed, 1924, Wrestling Featherweight, Gold

Ray Dodge, 1924, 800-meters, 6th

Ralph Spearow, 1924, Pole Vault, 6th

Russell Vis, 1924, Wrestling Lightweight, Gold

Arne Sundberg, 1928, Weightlifting team member; 1932, Weightlifting Lightweight, 5th

Joyce Macrae, 1940, Swimming, Games not held

Brenda Helser, 1940, Swimming, Games not held; 1948, 4x100 Freestyle Relay, Gold; 400-meter Freestyle, 5th

Nancy Merki, 1948, 400-meter Freestyle, 8th

Suzanne Zimmerman, 1948, 100-meter Backstroke, Silver

Herb Haberlach, 1952, Freestyle Wrestling Heavyweight, did not place

Maureen Murphy, 1956, 100-meter Backstroke, 5th

Lee Allen, Greco-Roman Wrestling Featherweight, did not place

Carolyn Wood, 1960, 4x100 Freestyle Relay, Gold; 100-meter Freestyle, 4th; 100-meter Butterfly, did not finish

Don Schollander, 1964, 100-meter Freestyle, Gold; 400-meter Freestyle, Gold; 4x100 Freestyle Relay, Gold; 4x200 Freestyle Relay, Gold; 1968, 200-meter Freestyle, Silver

Cathy Jamison, 1968, 200-meter Breaststroke, 5th

Richard "Rick" Sanders, 1968, Wrestling Flyweight, Silver; 1972, Wrestling Bantamweight, Silver

Henk Schenk, 1968, Greco-Roman Wrestling; 1972, Wrestling Heavyweight, did not place

Ken Patera, 1972, Weightlifting, did not place

Aldis Berzins, 1984, Volleyball, Gold

Carrie Steinseifer, 1984, 100-meter Freestyle, Gold (tie); 4x100 Freestyle Relay, Gold

These athletes were all products of the MAC and its coaches or, as members, they chose to compete in MAC colors.

ROD A. MOORE, ADAMS HESS MOORE • DR. W. GLYNN ROBERSON & FAMILY • DOUGLAS R
ANDERSON • KENNETH D. STEPHENS • NANCY STEPHENS • KIRK L. DIETRICK • DARCY ST
AMY & JULIE ENGELGAU • LAWRENCE W. & JANE B. HARRIS • BOB & DOROTHY HUNTER •
DAVIS • SHIRLEY & HERBERT SEMLER • SHELLI SEMLER • JILL & ERIC SEMLER • MATTHEW
STORCH CORPORATION ENGINEERS • WILLIAM B. BOONE • THE MALETIS FAMILY • LAM
• THE SWIGERT FAMILY • THE BOB GRANT FAMILY • THE STUART HALL FAMILY • WILSO
KUCKENBERG • ALEC RUNCIMAN • JANICE HOOSON • THE MORT BISHOP FAMILY • JOH
THE LOVETT FAMILY • MARY G. COLTON • ORVILLE & EDNA MAE BOYLE • DUANE C. LAWR
• ERIC R. CHRISTENSON FAMILY • ALLAN T.J. & LOIS M. McINNIS • ROY & BEVERLEY ELL
POORMAN FAMILIES • JON & JEAN ROTH • MRS. MYRTLE T. RUSSELL • LOWELL E., J. CHA
STAG • KELLY S. DOHERTY, FRYE COPYSYSTEM • HARRIET & H. STEWART TREMAINE • DOU
FAMILY • STEPHANIE GROOTENDORST • THE ROSLUND FAMILY • THE NOLES FAMILY • T
STACK FAMILY • THE GRAHAM COLTON FAMILY • DUDLEY STARR CO. • JOHN & NANCY HE
• CONNIE & SLUG PALMER • MACY, PAT, LAURA, KENT & CAROLINE WALL • THE ROGOVO
BOLAND • ORAN & MARGERY ROBERTSON • MARY P. ROWLAND & FAMILY • SCOTT, LINE
• THE VIRGIL CAVAGNARO FAMILY • THE ZIER FAMILY • PAUL TULACZ, D.V.M. • THE DE
THE HERBERT H. ANDERSON FAMILY • THE FREDRICKSON FAMILY • THE DON & LINDY BU
A. FEIRING • JOHN HELMER—FOUR GENERATIONS • AL, MINA & BARRY DISDERO • JOHN
NELSON • JOANNE & MARVIN McINTYRE • THE CLOSS FAMILY • MILES & MARY SWEENEY
• TOM ATIYEH & LESLIE SLOCUM • THE KEVIN KELLY FAMILY • THOMAS & JOYCE MACDON
CAMERON • THE STEVEN EASTERDAY FAMILY • LEE & DORIS MIESEN • DOUGLAS, DANIEL
• THE MURTAGH FAMILY • ANDREW & ADAM ALINEA TAITANO • ARTHUR G. BERGREEN •
R. GOODELL FAMILY • DOUG & BONNIE STROUD • DOUGLAS B. GORDON • DR. & MRS.
• GRETCHEN M. VETTO • HAROLD, ALEX & SUSAN RODINSKY • HERBERT B. COOPER • JIM
DAWSON FARR • LINDA & DAN POLLOCK • LIZ MILLER-BUTLER & JACK BUTLER • LOIS SI
• MARTHA GAY SKOIEN • MILTON JOHNSON, D.M.D., JOANN, B.A., M.A. • MIR FAMILY
RONALD B. GUSTAFF • STEWART G. STRAUS FAMILY • THE CONYARD FAMILY • THE D.O.
• THE FARRENS FAMILY • THE FLETCHER FAMILY • THE GEORGE F. BEALL FAMILY • THE M
• THE PEASE FAMILY • THE STANDRING FAMILY • THE TOM SHREWSBURY FAMILY • THE VIC
GOLDSMITH • EDWARD H. LOOK • THE BARRAGAR FAMILY • THE VIRGIL L. HAMLIN FAMILY
• ROGER & EVE BACHMAN • ROGER & MAGGIE MARTIN • THE R.W. VAN WINKLE FAMILY •
• DR. & MRS. SCOTT ANDERSON • THOMAS WRIGHTSON • NEWT, JANET & HILARY BAK
DONNA & LYDIA DELO • FRANKLIN GRIFFITH DRAKE • HILLMAN LUEDDEMANN JR
POBOCHENKO • NADINE MARIE ROBERTSON • HOWARD F. ROBERTSON • SHAUN STUART
D. HUEGLI & FAMILY • JOHN M. & PATRICIA M. O'BRIEN • THE GAREY FAMILY • JASON &
JAYN KELLAR • MERYL A. CONGER • THURBER FAMILY • RON, JO & DOUG BAILEY • JEAN
& J.J., LIBBY & CHRIS • PETER & LESLIE RICHTER • THE LARPENTEUR FAMILY • RALPH C